# NATIVE AMERICAN COLLEGES

A SPECIAL REPORT

# Native American Colleges

PROGRESS AND PROSPECTS

PAUL BOYER

AN ERNEST L. BOYER PROJECT OF
THE CARNEGIE FOUNDATION
FOR THE ADVANCEMENT OF TEACHING

5 IVY LANE, PRINCETON, NEW JERSEY 08540

LIBRARY OF CONGRESS CATALOGING-IN-PUBLICATION DATA

Boyer, Paul, 1964–
    Native American colleges : progress and prospects / Paul Boyer.
       p.   cm. — (A special report)
    "An Ernest L. Boyer project of the Carnegie Foundation for the Advancement of Teaching"—CIP t.p.
    Includes bibliographical references and index.
    ISBN 0–931050–63–4 (pbk. : alk. paper)
    1. Indian universities and colleges—United States.   I. Boyer, Ernest L.  II. Title.  III. Series: Special report (Carnegie Foundation for the Advancement of Teaching)
E97.55.B69  1997
378.73'08997–dc21                        97-13002

Copies are available from

JOSSEY-BASS INC., PUBLISHERS
350 Sansome Street, Fifth Floor
San Francisco, California 94104

PHONE (888) 378-2537   FAX (800) 605-2665

Visit our site on the World Wide Web:
http://www.carnegiefoundation.org

THIS CARNEGIE FOUNDATION REPORT was begun during the presidential tenure of Dr. Ernest L. Boyer, who died on December 8, 1995. It is published in grateful memory of his vision, his leadership, and his service.

# CONTENTS

EIGHT YEARS AGO, The Carnegie Foundation published *Tribal Colleges: Shaping the Future of Native America*. This special report introduced a new kind of college to the nation—institutions of higher learning founded by American Indians and, in most cases, located on reservations.

The report described a young movement facing an uncertain future. Small, poor, and geographically isolated, the tribally controlled colleges were a nearly invisible part of America's education landscape. The oldest of these institutions was celebrating its twentieth anniversary; most were started less than a decade before. All were located in the most rural and, often, poverty-stricken corners of the Northern Plains and Southwest, from the Blackfeet Reservation in northwest Montana to the heart of the Navajo Nation in Arizona.

Without adequate funding, they seemed to survive on sheer determination. Classes at many colleges were taught in leftover government buildings or old trailers set in wind-swept fields. Students—and teachers—parked their beat-up cars in gravel lots and did without most campus "extras," including faculty offices, cafeterias, student lounges, or well-stocked libraries.

But inside these makeshift campuses, their strengths—and real value—became clear. After visiting a half dozen colleges and talking with hundreds of students, faculty, administrators, and tribal leaders, I came to see how important tribal colleges were as symbols of hope. In communities still trying to cope with upheaval initiated hundreds of years earlier, a tribal college represented evidence of change and, possibly, a whole new era for Native Americans.

Even then, tribal colleges were making a difference. They had already graduated hundreds of students, mostly single mothers who never would have left the reservation to attend a non-Indian college. And most of these graduates had found work, often in reservations where unemployment reached 60 percent or more. Equally important, the colleges were rebuilding respect for traditional culture by teaching their languages, recording oral histories, and working with elders. They also responded to the most pressing social needs of their communities through programs ranging from literacy tutoring to substance abuse counseling.

The report documented this work and urged both public and private sectors to support the fledgling movement. The nation responded. Federal funding climbed significantly for several years. Corporate and foundation grants also grew. Meaningful partnerships were formed with non-Indian colleges and universities that benefited both faculty and students. Colleges and their leaders were featured on television programs and in national newspapers and magazines. It was an important turning point.

After the release of the report, I continued to write about the tribal college movement and saw, with each passing year, how the colleges were growing and changing. New institutions were created. Enrollments climbed. New degrees were added. Whole new approaches to teaching and community service were being devised. And, in the process, the tangible evidence of their success grew. The colleges were no longer curious experiments; their value was proven. They were not, as we wrote, "on the threshold of a new era." They were now, in many cases, mature, stable, and respected institutions of higher learning.

The Carnegie Foundation report remained an important resource, but it was an increasingly outdated document. So two years ago, the Foundation agreed to revisit the colleges and take note of their progress. This report is the result. Although it is built on the foundation of the original study—and one chapter, "A History of Mis-education," remains largely intact—it is a fundamentally new report. The data cited are among the most recent available, and the latest approaches to teaching are described. It also includes student opinions, collected from a Carnegie Foundation-sponsored survey of over 1,600 tribal college students from 24 campuses across the country.

As in the first report, we conclude with ten recommendations for action. Here we cite ample evidence of progress, but we also issue new calls to action. Once again, we say the federal responsibility to Native Americans must not be neglected. And we continue to believe support from the private sector remains vital to the growth of tribal colleges.

This report is unique in that never before has The Carnegie Foundation returned so soon to the same group of institutions to reaffirm its confidence in their work. To do so now reflects, certainly, the special needs of tribal colleges. Their survival depends on continued—and constant—support from the nation. A few brief moments of fame are not enough; real change happens over time.

But it must be stressed that this report exists because of Ernest Boyer. As president of The Carnegie Foundation until his death in December 1995, he made tribal colleges a special priority. He passionately believed that the nation continues to have a moral responsibility to America's native peoples and he freely shared the Foundation's resources and credibility with a group of institutions that had, at the time, little of either. He never saw this final report, but it is part of his special legacy to American education.

# ACKNOWLEDGMENTS

THIS CARNEGIE FOUNDATION report represents nearly two years of work, and reflects the talents of a truly diverse group of people. We must first thank the network of twenty-seven tribally controlled colleges. Presidents, faculty, staff, and students supported this project by offering the information—and inspiration—needed to make it possible.

Before writing The Carnegie Foundation's first report on tribal colleges in 1989, we toured seven campuses, spending several days at each. This time, we took a slightly different approach by spending three months on one tribal college campus—Salish Kootenai College on the Flathead Indian Reservation of western Montana. This institution, led by president Joseph McDonald, helped us appreciate the real importance of tribal colleges to the lives of students and the future of reservation communities. By attending classes, talking to students, participating in the day-to-day life of the college and surrounding community, our respect for this institution—and all tribal colleges—grew even deeper. The college deserves special recognition.

For a broader perspective, we also talked with educators and community leaders working with tribes and Indian organizations across the country. Patrick Head, Jack Barden, Cheryl Crazy Bull, Judy Gobert, Wayne Stein, Schuyler Houser, and Jerry Reynolds were among those consulted for their special knowledge of tribal development needs.

Many presidents took time to review early drafts of the report. The comments resulted in a more accurate and relevant document. We would like to thank Bob Lorence, Janine Pease Pretty-On-Top, Jim Shanley, Joseph McDonald, Richard Little Bear, and Tommy Lewis for their thoughtful critiques. These and other presidents and staff also contributed informally throughout the writing and editing process.

Staff at the American Indian Higher Education Consortium, including director Veronica Gonzales, Leyna McConkey, and Jason Gavin, supplied data and an understanding of the federal role in Indian education. At the American Indian College Fund, Shannon Finley and Barbara Bratone helped us appreciate the importance of private sector support to reservations. As editor of the tribal colleges' journal, Marjane Ambler provided contacts and a wealth of information about the colleges and their many accomplishments.

Support from Carnegie Foundation staff was essential. Mary Jean Whitelaw helped produce a survey distributed to 1,600 tribal college students, and analyzed the results. She was assisted in this work by Lois Harwood and Craig Wacker. These data add significantly to our understanding of tribal colleges.

Jan Hempel also deserves special thanks. She helped edit the final manuscript and guided it expertly through the production process. Her enthusiasm and skill made this process—usually an unpleasant chore—truly enjoyable. Johanna Wilson worked methodically to keep the report on schedule and hold all of the pieces together. Dawn Berberian, with her usual efficiency and accuracy, performed the word processing. Bob Hochstein, a dear friend, took hold of the completed report and carried its message to the world.

Charles Glassick, interim president of The Carnegie Foundation, supported the report and encouraged it to move forward, even during a period of transition at the Foundation. His careful attention to this project was vital to its success.

To my father, Ernest Boyer, this report is dedicated. He made it all possible.

# Symbols of a New Era

THE STORY of Native Americans[1] is told, almost always, in the language of despair. Indian life is filled with images of poverty, and government policy has consistently been called a failure. We often speak of "the plight of the Indian" and conclude with resignation that little can be done.

But much is already being done. In a movement still hidden from most of the nation, hope and a sense of renewal has emerged in American Indian communities. With determination, many Native Americans are working to rekindle lost cultural values, restore a sense of community, and find practical solutions to the needs of their tribal nations. With growing confidence they are finding economic, political, spiritual, and intellectual strength that had been discredited or actively suppressed for generations.

The evidence of this movement is seen on reservations across the nation. Exerting more control over their own communities and eager to have a voice in national affairs, America's indigenous peoples are making their presence felt more strongly now than ever. American Indians are learning to make their case and address their own needs. In the courts, in the press, and in the halls of Congress, Native American voices are being heard.

But education is, as always, the key to social renewal, and without question the most significant development in American Indian communities since World War II was the creation of tribally controlled colleges, institutions of higher learning founded by tribes and governed by Indians. More than any other single institution, they are changing lives and offering real hope for the future.

Although the oldest tribal college was started less than thirty years ago, these fledgling institutions are remaking the educational and social landscapes of America's reservations. They are challenging economic stagnation and aggressively confronting the devastating impact of alcoholism and drug abuse. Of equal importance, they are reaffirming tribal traditions that were slipping away.

And their impact is real. Research, site visits, accreditation reports, and government audits all confirm their effectiveness. Tribal colleges have proven their ability to enroll students who were not served by higher education, to graduate students who had dropped out from other institutions, and to sponsor successful community development programs. They have also proven their ability to responsibly manage themselves as institutions, gaining the respect of Washington lawmakers and private foundations. No less remarkable has been the ability of most to gain acceptance within their own communities and to navigate through the shifting winds of tribal politics. Indeed, the tribal college is often the most stable institution on a reservation.

Overwhelming problems still exist on most reservations. One institution alone cannot break down all the barriers Indians face. American Indian communities remain isolated, chronically neglected places that benefit little from the nation's wealth. Unemployment and alcoholism are persistent problems in these forgotten regions, and statistics on life expectancy, family income, and educational opportunities among Native Americans can parallel those of Third World countries.

But after years of physical hardship and cultural neglect, Indians themselves are again gaining the confidence and skills needed to lead their nations. A new mood of optimism and self-respect among native people has emerged and the results are starting to show.

THE FIRST TRIBAL COLLEGE opened in 1968 on the Navajo Reservation. As Navajos began to assert their rights more aggressively, there was frustration that few tribal members had the skills needed to effectively lead a nation with a population reaching two hundred thousand. Leaders—including Guy Gorman, Dean C. Jackson and others—recognized that higher education was a key to self-determination.

Three decades later, Navajo Community College graduated close to ten thousand students and currently enrolls about fifteen hundred. Its main campus is located in the geographic center of the reservation, but the college has grown to include a sister campus in Shiprock, New Mexico, and five satellite campuses.

Today there are twenty-seven tribally controlled colleges in eleven states—from California to Michigan, and from Arizona to North Dakota. Together these institutions enroll approximately twenty thousand students from over two hundred tribes and indigenous groups.[2] And the movement continues to grow. New colleges are being founded, primarily along a band stretching from Alaska to the Great Lakes region, where the desire for education is high but opportunities are believed to be limited. In addition, most colleges—especially the youngest—are growing between 10 and 100 percent a year.

But the challenges the colleges confront cannot be overstated. A typical tribal college necessarily charges low tuition but lacks a tax base to support the full cost of the education provided. Meanwhile, the limited federal support these institutions receive—the backbone of their funding—fails to keep pace with enrollment growth.

The colleges are working with growing success to find other sources of support. All raise money privately and take advantage of government and foundation grants. Increasingly, the colleges also share resources among themselves. Since the founding of the American Indian College Fund in 1989, private donations and foundation grants have allowed the colleges to build an endowment and distribute scholarship money to students. The American Indian Higher Education Consortium's office outside Washington, D.C., has allowed the colleges to learn about and take part in a wide range of government-funded programs sponsored by departments as diverse as Defense and Agriculture. Out of necessity, the tribal college administrators and staff have become among the most politically aware in higher education.

These are hopeful signs, but success is relative. Only a few years ago, tribal colleges found support from a small number of regional foundations and many existed almost entirely on a single congressional appropriation. Some colleges wondered if they would survive for another semester. Today, the future seems more secure, but the colleges remain chronically underfunded and unrecognized, operating with fewer dollars per student than most other colleges or universities in America.

Considering the enormously difficult conditions tribal colleges endure, with resources most collegiate institutions would find unacceptably restrictive, their impact is remarkable. It became unmistakably clear during our initial visits that, even as they struggle to fulfill their mandates, tribal colleges are crucial to the future of Native American societies, and of our nation. After seven years of further observation, this belief has been confirmed, and is renewed.

*First, tribal colleges establish a learning environment that supports students who had come to view failure as the norm.* The attrition rate among Indian students, at both the school and college levels, greatly exceeds the rate for white students.[3] According to a 1993 report by the American Council on Education, "American Indians persist in college at the lowest rate of all postsecondary entrants." It concluded that "only 30 percent of all American Indians who enroll at four-year colleges graduate within six years."[4] More recent reports by ACE found a rise in enrollment and graduation rates in the early 1990s. But Native Americans continue to trail black, Hispanic, and Asian American students.[5] Isolated by distance and culture, many have come to accept that they cannot complete school. College seems to many Native Americans an impossible dream. Tribal colleges offer hope in this climate of despair.

Most of the colleges offer tutoring programs that build basic skills, and also provide active counseling programs for their students. Faculty and administrators reach out to students having trouble or missing classes. And without sacrificing academic rigor, courses are often tailored to reflect the unique learning styles of American Indian students. Students confirm the value of this attention, reporting to us that tribal colleges are friendlier and more supportive institutions.

*Second, tribal colleges celebrate and help sustain Native American traditions.* For many Americans, Indian culture is little more than images of teepees, peace pipes, and brightly colored rugs. But in many reservation communities, traditional cultural values remain a vital part of the social fabric. Tribal languages are still spoken, and traditional beliefs are respected.

While non-Indian schools and colleges have long ignored Indian culture, tribal colleges view it as their curricular center. They argue that it is through a reconnection to these long-standing cultural skills and beliefs that Indians can build a strong self-image and participate, with confidence, in the dominant society. Each of the tribal colleges offers courses, sometimes taught by tribal elders, in native languages, history, philosophy, and the arts, botany, astronomy, and more.

Traditional values such as cooperation and respect for elders are embedded in the culture of these institutions. Differing ideas about how time should be managed and how people should interact with each other are understood and accepted. In mainstream institutions, Indians can find their own values undermined; tribal colleges, in contrast, reinforce the values of Indian culture.

*Third, tribal colleges provide essential services that enrich surrounding communities.* These colleges are, in the truest sense, community institutions. Most are located on reservations, and all offer social and economic programs for tribal advancement. Literacy tutoring, high school equivalency programs, alcohol and substance abuse counseling are a vital part of most colleges. Others work cooperatively with local businesses and industries to build a stronger economic base. Increasingly, they help community members start and finance their own businesses.

Tribal colleges also bring information and new ideas into their communities. They hold community forums, allowing the tribal members to gather in a politically neutral setting for discussion of issues critical to their future. They also sponsor the arts—both traditional and modern— bringing performers onto reservations and celebrating local talent. One college also sponsors a television station and another has recently established a public radio station, both serving rural areas far from other media outlets. Navajo Community College sponsors a Native American arts festival, cultural workshop, and much more.

*Fourth, the colleges have become centers for research and scholarship.* Increasingly, the colleges are working with non-Indian universities, research institutes, and government agencies, taking part in studies of economic development, teaching methodology, tribal leadership, the environment, and other issues critical to tribal development.

With growing confidence, the colleges are also developing their own research agendas. One college, for example, brings graduate psychology students to its institution, where they teach, offer counseling services, and—with college guidance—study mental health issues.[6] Other colleges are investigating barriers to Indian achievement in math and science, or finding new ways to teach advanced math courses. Little Big Horn College is performing biodiversity studies on prairie grasslands with two federal departments. The colleges' journal, meanwhile, features the scholarship generated by the colleges and Indian researchers.

In a new initiative, the colleges are also formally defining scholarship for themselves, asking such questions as: What is Indian scholarship? What is the relevance of Western science to Indian scholarship? The emphasis is on rebuilding respect for traditional ways of knowing. American Indian cultures find strength through their language, kinship, and a strong sense of connection to nature and the cosmos—and these subjects may be more satisfactorily investigated and understood through forms of scholarship distinctly Indian.

These institutions have taken on a breathtaking array of responsibilities. With each passing year, tribal colleges prove their worth to tribal communities, and to the nation. They can no longer be dismissed as risky experiments, nor can their accomplishments be ignored. They are a permanent part of their reservations and this country.

We believe it is a moment of great opportunity for the colleges and for the United States. For hundreds of years, this nation failed to address the critical needs of American Indians. Many efforts were misguided disasters and almost all were failures. Today, tribal colleges are offering the reservations and tribal communities the chance to build knowledge, skills, confidence, and pride in a way not possible for non-Indian institutions to offer. By recognizing, and rewarding, the accomplishments and contributions of these unique institutions, the nation will help them to do even more—and everyone will share in their success.

# CHAPTER I

# *A History of Mis-education*

AMERICA'S MAINSTREAM COLLEGES have enrolled Indians for over 350 years. From the time of the first English settlement, Native Americans have been encouraged to participate in this ritual of Western civilization. But the goal was almost always assimilation, seldom the enhancement of the Indian students or the well-being of their tribes.

In 1619, the fragile Jamestown settlement in Virginia was only tenuously rooted in the New World. Still, at the first Assembly of Burgesses, "workmen of all sorts" were urged to contribute their skills "for the erecting of [a] university and college."[1] When the East India School opened its doors in 1621, included in the first student body were Indian children from the local tribe.

A commentator of the time put the purposes for enrolling Indians this way: "It would be proper to draw the best disposed among the Indians to converse and labor with our people for a convenient reward that they might not only learn a civil way of life, but be brought to a knowledge of religion and become instruments in the conversion of their countrymen."[2]

While the East India School's charter called for the education of Indian boys "in the first elements of literature," missionary work was a more urgent motivation. It was expected that Indian students would embrace the Christian faith and carry on "the work of conversion" after graduation. These hopes were soon dashed, however, when in 1622 the superintendent of the East India School and some residents were killed during an Indian uprising. The fledgling college closed.

Harvard College, founded in 1636, listed among its goals "the Education of the English and Indian youth of this country in knowledge and Goodness" and created a special college-within-a-college, for "twenty

Indian pupils."[3] The response was disappointing. Few young Indians ever went to Harvard, and many of those who did enter the college did not stay.

Illness and death, as well as the curriculum of Latin and the Western classics, weeded out all but the hardiest and most determined Indian scholars. Here is how one observer described the roadblocks at Harvard College: "For several of the said youth died, after they had been sundry years at learning, and made good proficiency therein. Others were disheartened and left learning, after they were almost ready for the college. And some returned to live among their countrymen."[4]

Dartmouth College was also inspired to educate and Christianize the Indians, as was the College of William and Mary. According to its charter, William and Mary was "to teach the Indian boys to read and write. . . . And especially to teach them thoroughly the catechism and the principles of the Christian religion."[5] But again, these intentions were never realized at the levels college founders had expected.

Still the American colonies tried, for more than 150 years, to incorporate the native population into the transplanted European education system. Young Indians were expected to change, and if they could not or would not meet the standards of European education, it was considered *their* failing, not the institution's. But there was little enthusiasm among Indians for English-style learning, and year after year there were few positive results.

At the time of the American Revolution, Indians were being dismissed as unwilling—or unable—to adapt to white society. With little allowance for cultural diversity, Americans began to feel pity or contempt when the natives failed to embrace Western culture. While some considered Indians "inherently equal" in a rather abstract fashion, there was among many others a scornful rejection of Native American values and beliefs.[6]

In 1785, Thomas Jefferson, reflecting perhaps the most enlightened view of the time, declared "the Indian to be in body and mind equal to the white man."[7] Yet in conversation with Indian groups sometime later, Jefferson was equally adamant in his promotion of European culture. "We shall with great pleasure," he proposed, "see your people become disposed to cultivate the earth, to raise herds of useful animals, and to spin and weave, for their food and clothing. These resources are certain, they will never disappoint you, while those of hunting may fail, and expose your women and children to the miseries of hunger and cold. We will with pleasure furnish you with implements of the most necessary arts, and with persons who may instruct [you] how to make and use them."[8]

Some Indians eagerly sought to learn the trades that they believed might offer them parity with the white invaders. Most, however, argued that Jefferson's world had little to offer Indian society and that Western education was, in fact, a destructive force. Benjamin Franklin, in 1794, recorded one Indian leader's analysis of Western education's poor performance among his people:

> But you, who are wise, must know that different Nations have different Conceptions of things; and you will therefore not take it amiss, if our ideas of this kind of Education happen not to be the same with yours. We have had some Experience of it; Several of our young people were formally brought up at the College of the Northern Provinces; they were instructed in all your Sciences; but, when they came back to us, they were bad Runners, ignorant of every means of living in the Woods, unable to bear either Cold or Hunger, knew neither how to build a Cabin, take a Deer, or kill an Enemy, spoke our Language imperfectly, were therefore neither fit for Hunters, Warriors, not Counselors, they were totally good for nothing. We are however not the less oblig'd by your kind Offer, tho' we decline accepting it; and, to show our grateful Sense of it, the Gentlemen of Virginia will send us a Dozen of their Sons, we will take great Care of their Education, instruct them in all we know, and make *Men* of them.[9]

As America pushed west, more and more Indian groups were physically subdued, and military leaders and civilians who followed in the wake of the American armed conquest often spoke disparagingly of what they saw in Indian communities, doubting the existence of a culture worth preserving. Prior to his becoming America's foremost landscape architect, Frederick Law Olmsted traveled through Texas and wrote his observations in detail. Visiting a group of Lipans in 1856, Olmsted reported: "Here . . . was nothing but the most miserable squalor, foul obscenity, and disgusting brutishness, if there be excepted the occasional evidence of a sly and impish keenness. We could not find even one man of dignity. . . ."[10]

Harsh judgments about Indian intelligence were common. Charles Maclaren, a fellow of the Royal Society of Edinburgh, reported in 1875, for example, that American Indians "are not only averse to the restraints of education but are for the most part incapable of a continued process of reasoning on abstract subjects. Their inventive and imitative faculties appear to be of very humble capacity, nor have they the smallest taste for the arts and sciences."[11]

In the aftermath of military struggles in the western lands during the early post–Civil War period, treaties were signed with the various tribes. The immediate goal was to give white settlers more land to control. But each document contained provisions intended both to subdue the Indians and transform their cultures. Often grants were provided through these documents for the promotion of education and for the introduction of white civilization through such artifacts as mills and blacksmith shops.

Again promises were broken. Few of the educational commitments were fulfilled. Some schools were built, but they were small and scattered. Since the *public* effort to educate the Indian children remained erratic and largely unsuccessful, the responsibility shifted largely to missionary groups. Early in the century, the Civilization Act of 1816 gave money for religious groups to promote Christianization and education among Indian tribes. While leadership differed, the assimilation goals of both the public and private schools were much the same.

As Indians were driven farther and farther from population centers, "reformers" began to call for complete integration of Indians into American culture. On the belief that Native Americans could best be served through their full absorption into the white world, schools were founded to provide a necessary bridge. In this era, publicly supported, off-reservation boarding schools were started. It was believed that children could be more easily educated if they were removed from their families and communities.

Richard Henry Pratt, an Army captain, was the most enthusiastic champion of this new educational philosophy. Granted use of an old army barracks in Pennsylvania by Congress, Pratt founded, in 1879, the Carlisle Indian School, where he gathered together two hundred Indian children and young adults from different Western tribes for academic and vocational learning, as well as socialization, built around a rigid daily schedule that included considerable physical labor. Pratt envisioned enough "Carlisles" to accommodate *all* Indian children. It was, he believed, the only way to make "real Americans" out of Indians. Such a view was generally seen as impractical, but the philosophical underpinnings were, nonetheless, consistent with the best hopes of policymakers.

Advocating complete submersion in white culture, Pratt made every effort at Carlisle to separate Indian students from their own heritage, including language. Use of English was mandatory at all times and violators were punished. Traditional Indian dress was not acceptable. Long hair on men was cut. Any evidence of attachment by students to their own cultures was viewed as an act of defiance. In his memoirs, Pratt noted, "I believe in immersing the Indians in our civilization and when we get them under, holding them there until they are thoroughly soaked."[12]

Religion continued to be a powerful force in Indian education efforts. Elaine Eastman, a sympathetic biographer of Pratt, noted in this regard: "Character-building through work and other wholesome discipline was reinforced by simple, nonsectarian religious teaching, the girls in small groups by members of the school faculty, the boys dispatched on Sunday mornings to different churches in town for wider experience."[13]

Carlisle and similar boarding schools were viewed by their advocates as institutions of hope and inspiration. By the turn of the century, there were twenty-five boarding schools, and amid the general ignorance and fear found in the white population, leaders at these schools argued that Native Americans deserved academic opportunity and could succeed, even excel, if motivated. Pratt believed that, with kind but firm guidance, "the mantle of citizenship will fit and sit comfortably upon [the American Indian]."[14]

Pratt's belief in the capacity of Indians to learn was, for that era, an enlightened vision. But within a few decades of Carlisle's founding, the failure of assimilation was clear. Here, as elsewhere, living conditions and the quality of education were often very poor. Discipline was harsh, and with limited federal funding, much of each student's day involved manual labor needed just to maintain the campus. Pratt called the work "character-building." In 1915, however, the Commissioner of Indian Affairs admitted that without the free labor of their students the schools could not be maintained, as Congress had not appropriated enough money for that purpose.

The missionary boarding schools were similar to Carlisle in their approach to education. One young woman, a student at a Catholic mission school in western Montana during this era, recalled the structured daily routine:

> With breakfast over, the long line of girls marched to the recreation room. From here each departed to perform her daily task. This duty was called "our charge." Depending on our age, it could be dusting the schoolrooms, or tearfully trying to build the fire with green cottonwood. There were long, cold corridors to sweep; wide, winding stairways to polish; parlors to arrange and a recreation room to put in order. . . . These and many other undertakings were accomplished before the school bell rang at nine o'clock.[15]

One gets the impression that this school was more concerned about hygiene than education.

Dropout rates at Indian boarding schools were always high—young students, to stay in school, had to be away from home and family for long periods of time. For the minority that did graduate, there was little chance for advancement either on or off the reservation. The Indians who passed through these schools were no longer considered a part of their tribal culture. Further, there were few jobs, since most graduates were trained for work not available on reservations. The complaints recorded years before by Benjamin Franklin remained unresolved.

The curriculum at both the boarding and the reservation schools stressed basic work skills. In the meager academic program that was offered, the rich heritage of the various tribes was rarely mentioned. In 1915, a new federal curriculum was proposed for all government-run Indian schools. It allotted time for English, arithmetic, geology, hygiene, and even breathing exercises, but included only one reference to Native American culture. The introduction to the syllabus suggested that "Indian methods of hand weaving" *might* be incorporated into art lessons.[16]

There was, in the new course of study, a suggested reading list that included "Little Red Riding Hood," "The Three Bears," "Peter Rabbit," and "The Hare and the Tortoise." A full complement of Mother Goose rhymes was also recommended. Missing was any mention of the great tradition of storytelling, so much a part of Native American culture.

The history curriculum is even more revealing. Beginning with Columbus's "discovery" in 1492, the focus remained solely on the transplanted European culture, with a celebration of its spread across the continent. Wars and territorial expansion were recalled in great detail, all from the new settlers' perspective. No mention was made of the impact of the invasion from the Indians' perspective, and no reference to the heartache and upheavals of such conquests.

This distortion of history was no accident. Thomas Morgan, Commissioner of Indian Affairs during the late 1800s, argued strongly that educators should instill patriotism in their Native American pupils and believed that teachers should "carefully avoid any unnecessary references to the fact that they are Indians."[17]

To live among whites, Indians were expected to become white. In an uncompromising society, Native American students were forced to embrace European life and renounce their own culture. Such a choice left deep scars. Many students were forced into a cultural no-man's-land, where they remained torn between two worlds, suffering deeply from the schism.

The failures of the national government's policies—both educational and economic—had a profound impact on all of Indian society. "At the beginning of the twentieth century," writes historian Margaret Szasz, "the status of the Indian was not only bleak, it was hovering on the edge of disaster."[18] Unskilled and powerless, Native Americans fell into a pattern of dependency.

Rather than promoting self-sufficiency, government policies created a seemingly endless cycle of dependency and despair. The victims, once again, were blamed. Government agents, who had driven Indians to arid tracts of land and offered inappropriate training, would then return, years later, to berate their charges for becoming despondent and dependent on government rations.

Self-sufficiency was the presumed goal of federally sponsored Indian education, but quite the opposite was accomplished. According to Francis Paul Prucha, a scholar of Native American policy, "the old was destroyed, but the new was not fully accepted, leaving many Indians in a kind of limbo and fostering the spirit of dependency."[19]

This bankrupt policy reached its lowest depths of hypocrisy and inaction at the turn of the century. Signs of failure were everywhere apparent and in response, a movement for fundamental reform slowly began to take root. In 1928, there came a catalyst for action with the release of what became known as the Meriam Report. Sponsored by the privately controlled Institute for Government Research, this bold critique took a comprehensive look at Indians in American society and confirmed, in vivid language, that conditions among Native Americans had deteriorated horribly.

In the introductory chapter of his report, Lewis Meriam noted:

> An overwhelming majority of Indians are poor, even extremely poor. . . . The income of the typical Indian family is low and the earned income extremely low. . . . The number of Indians who are supporting themselves through their own efforts, according to what a white man would regard as the minimum standard of health and decency, is extremely small. . . . Many of them are living on lands from which a trained and experienced white man could scarcely wrest a reasonable living.[20]

Two days after the report's release, a *New York Times* editorial agreed with the document's central argument, lamenting that ". . . our relations with the Indians during the last few decades have been characterized by good intentions without a sympathetic understanding of the Indian's needs, and that we have done little of a practical nature to help them adapt themselves to the conditions which they have to face."[21]

In its critique of Indian education, the Meriam Report focused on government-run boarding schools. Although by the 1920s boarding schools provided for the education of only about one quarter of the total Indian student population, the report focused on these institutions as symbols of the need for fundamental change. The study offered detailed evidence of mismanagement and physical abuse at these institutions, reporting that, at times, students were provided a diet that guaranteed only slow starvation. Military order, harsh discipline, and poorly trained teachers also were criticized.

Looking at the curriculum, the Meriam Report charged that government-run schools were not providing skills relevant to Indians. It was argued that curricula in these schools were too uniform, that they stressed only white culture and ignored the many cultural differences found among tribes. The report argued that "Indian tribes and individual Indians within the tribes vary so greatly that standard content and methods of education would be worse than futile."[22]

The report also attacked the heavy emphasis on vocational training that often closed rather than opened doors. The trades offered were in areas with little chance for employment, and the detachment of the training from Indian culture left students isolated from their heritage. The addition of Indian culture into the curricula would, the report argued, reduce this unnecessary separation.

The Meriam Report had instant impact. Six months after its release, the *New York Times* summarized the new mood. "It is time to consider a question of principle," the editorial began. "Is it right to continue the policy of trying to de-Indianize the Indians and make white men out of them?"[23] Within five years, twelve boarding schools had closed or changed to daytime schools, and some schools had introduced programs encouraging Indians themselves to teach native arts.

Following the election of Franklin Roosevelt in 1932, the pace of reform quickened. John Collier was appointed Commissioner of Indian Affairs. A scholar of Indian culture and advocate of community-based education, Collier was determined to shape government policies on the basis of *Indian* needs, not on the basis of what whites wanted Indians to become. Under his leadership, the next twelve years brought sweeping and historic changes in Indian education policy.

First, Collier redefined the federal government's relationship with Native Americans. He argued that "Indian societies, whether ancient, regenerated or created anew, must be given status, responsibility and power."[24] In response to this fresh thought, the Indian Reorganization Act was passed by Congress in 1934. Designed to reverse the devastation of long-standing policy, the new legislation focused on safeguarding Native American sovereignty. Among the four key provisions in the bill were commitments to Indian self-government, the consolidation of Indian land holdings, economic development on the reservations, and support for cultural pluralism—the restoration of cultural traditions. Self-determination, for the first time, became a centerpiece of Indian policy.

In the new legislation, education was considered crucial, but this time the goal was to free students, not suppress them. Collier wanted an education program in which Indians would gain skills to lead and also be prepared to earn a living. No longer viewed as subordinates in white society, Indians were to be empowered both to sustain their traditional culture and negotiate increasingly complex government–Indian relationships. "The grant of freedom," he argued, "must be more . . . than a remission of enslavement."[25]

Community schools became the focus of the Bureau's new perspective. No longer committed to indoctrination, these institutions were to be community service centers, offering much more than the three R's. In arid regions, for example, the drinking water and bath houses of the new schools were accessible to all. Repair shops at the schools became available for adult use, and patronage of the libraries by everyone was encouraged. In all community schools, curricula became more flexible, and courses in Indian culture were introduced. A new day had dawned.

Still, attitudes had to change. Although many educators had worked with Indian children for years, there was considerable ignorance of the culture and lack of respect for traditional beliefs. In-service training for teachers in the reservation schools was also offered, and in special summer institutes, teachers studied Indian culture and considered ways to be more responsive to student needs.

There was also a short-lived program to prepare Indians to be teachers. The need for role models—persons who could live as Indians and also appreciate the dominant culture—became a priority. (The project was canceled during World War II after having prepared only fifty Native American instructors.)

The 1930s was a time of new vision and bold experimentation. Important changes were made, but the era was short. At the close of the decade, fundamental issues remained unresolved. The Great Depression limited the money available for innovative programs and slowed the push for overhaul and reform.

The Bureau of Indian Affairs was still unable to reassure young Indians that it was acceptable to learn about their roots, and even the enlightened schools could not, according to historian Margaret Szasz, "begin to solve the problems of adjustment for a disoriented Indian child. A course in silverwork or in Indian history did not answer the child's question: Who am I?"[26]

Further, in spite of the new enlightenment, the Indian voice was rarely heard. Policies controlling reservations and schools were still determined mostly by white administrators. Even those advocating reform apparently failed to see the irony in having outsiders design programs that sought Indian self-determination.

Barriers notwithstanding, many new insights were, in fact, achieved. It was now realized, for example, that the unique values and heritage of Indian people could not be discarded in the pursuit of assimilation. A new set of policies emerged, based on the acceptance of cultural variation and Native American self-government. While education programs did not fully meet the needs of Indian society or accept Indians as full policymaking partners, a new era had clearly begun. Collier's vision and Roosevelt's Indian New Deal are still felt today.

Reformist energy was lost as World War II shifted the priorities of the nation. Programs were cut and funding was reduced. Reflecting a manpower shortage throughout the country, the Indian Service suffered from a loss of teachers and students as both went to work elsewhere or to join the Armed Services.

But a renewed emphasis on higher education was about to take place, and the Civil Rights era would look kindly on the unique needs and talents of minority groups, including Indians. The stage was set for the founding of the first tribal colleges.

# CHAPTER II

# The Founding of Tribal Colleges

I N 1911, an Indian named August Breuninger proposed the creation of an Indian university that would focus on Native American culture and be connected to an Indian museum.[1] In a letter outlining his proposal, Breuninger argued that such an institution would both create opportunity for Indians and demonstrate the vitality of Indian culture:

> A University for Indians is the greatest step that we educated Indians could make in uniting our people . . . It would eliminate the general conception—that an Indian consists of only feathers and paint. It would single us out—as REALLY PROGRESSIVE INDIANS. It would give us a better influence with the rising generation, by setting out our character in such a conspicuous manner as to be . . . observed and imitated by them.[2]

Advocates of an Indian-controlled college were not looking to retreat from the modern world; rather, they hoped higher education would allow Indians to participate fully in American society. It was not surprising, however, that strict assimilationists of the period opposed such efforts. Richard Pratt, for example, believed Indian-controlled education would work against their integration into American society. As founder of the Carlisle Indian School, he reflected some of the most enlightened thinking of the time, yet he firmly held that Indian culture was, by definition, a hindrance to advancement.

Against this prevailing attitude, proposals for native colleges continued to be made periodically for another half century, but with little result. The early enthusiasm of colonists and missionaries who tried to establish colleges for Indians disappeared. Instead, attention shifted to training for vocational occupations, with little expectation that students would proceed further.

Opportunities for Indians did exist, but were limited. Prior to World War II, some boarding schools provided college preparatory instruction and after release of the Meriam Report a growing number of universities and colleges offered scholarships to Indian students. Several federal loan programs were also established.[3]

However, overwhelming barriers remained in place. Poor preparation and high dropout rates in earlier grades kept Indians from college, cultural differences remained unaddressed, and only a limited number of loans and scholarships were offered. In addition, Indian students were often discouraged from attending college by their own teachers who, inspired by misguided kindness or overt racism, did not want to see their students enter the more rigorous life of higher education where, in their view, failure was likely.[4]

By the start of World War II, many tribes had yet to see any of their members earn a college degree. There were Native Americans who had achieved at the highest level, becoming doctors, theologians, politicians, and national education leaders, but their numbers were disproportionately small.[5] A few years of formal education—under the watchful eye of the federal government or church groups—was all that was available, or expected, for most Native Americans.

After World War II, however, two key events came together and led, in 1968, to the founding of the first tribal college. There was a dramatic shift in the federal government's Indian policy, first to "termination" then to "self-determination." Termination made many Indian leaders aware of their vulnerability to government capriciousness, while self-determination gave them resources needed to create their own institutions and define their own policies.

## From Termination to Self-determination

By the mid-1940s, the reformist energy of the New Deal was lost and, suddenly, Congress began talking about getting out of the "Indian business." A new policy of termination was promoted that would eliminate reservations by parceling out the land to individual tribal members and shift many Indian programs to the states. Free to keep or sell land once held in trust, Indians would no longer be wards of the federal government and would become—politically at least—indistinguishable from all other Americans.

Advocates of termination argued that they were not abandoning Indians, but were setting them free. Ironically, they cited the heroism of Indian GIs, explaining that their contribution in wartime should be rewarded with "emancipation" from reservation life and BIA interference. Some even compared reservations to concentration camps.[6]

By the early 1950s opposition to termination increased and, most tribes slated for termination never were. But for those removed from the list of federally recognized tribes, the impact was devastating. Ada Deer, a Mennominee, called her tribe's termination "a cultural, economic, and political disaster." She continued:

> It is going to take several more generations for the people in my tribe to recover from the damage that was done during termination. The hospital and the roads were closed. Our land became subject to taxation. A whole new county, Wisconsin's poorest county, was created as a result of this."[7]

Washington quickly retreated from immediate termination and devised plans that would more gently prepare reservations for termination through economic development. Yet most of these programs were clumsy, ineffective, and sometimes even harmful.

Industries were offered incentives to relocate onto reservations, but few did. Meanwhile a massive human relocation program moved some 125,000 unemployed Indians from reservations to large urban centers. The promises were expansive—good housing, education, a good job, and prosperity—but the reality was devastating. Job training was inadequate, economic conditions were poor, and little was done to address the isolation and discrimination the transplanted Indians endured. Finding little support, many Indians simply went back home; relocatees returned at the rate of 30 percent in the first three months of placement.[8]

Out of the wreckage of termination, a new policy emerged calling for greater Indian self-determination. In a Special Message called "The Forgotten American," President Johnson declared in 1968 that the federal government must now be committed to "a policy of maximum choice for the American Indian: a policy expressed in programs of self-help, self-development, self-determination."[9] President Nixon carried the policy through the early 1970s and it has been endorsed by every administration since.[10]

Self-determination has not eliminated federal responsibility to American Indians. Indeed, it brought a renewed commitment to Indians. According to a 1968 Senate Concurrent Resolution, Congress pledged to support "a policy of developing the necessary programs and services to bring Indian and Alaskan natives to a desirable social and economic level of fully participating citizens." This policy became law in 1975 with the Self-Determination Act, which funded technical training, BIA staff support, and required the government to contract federal programs to tribes wanting to assume greater control.

While many termination-era programs were abandoned, new ones took their place. And, of special importance, existing appropriations for a wide range of Great Society programs, such as Manpower Development Training, Head Start, and Area Redevelopment, were made available to Indian communities. Native Americans became constituents of all federal departments and no longer relied exclusively on the Bureau of Indian Affairs.[11]

For tribes, these changes offered new opportunities, but they also required new skills. The machinations of the federal bureaucracy had to be learned. New programs had to be administered and accounted for. The expertise of lawyers, lobbyists, and grant writers became necessary. Suddenly, much more was expected of tribes, and much more money was at stake.

## THE NEED FOR HIGHER EDUCATION

The value of higher education became clear to many American Indian leaders in this new era of self-determination. A college degree did not have to be synonymous with assimilation. Now it could be used to strengthen reservations and tribal culture. This belief that higher education could serve the practical needs of a tribe was the second ingredient necessary for the founding of the tribal college.

It also reflected the changing status of higher education in the nation as a whole. After World War II, the GI Bill encouraged millions of returning soldiers to enroll in college and America's campuses swelled with first-generation students. Passage of the Higher Education Act in 1965 made a college education even more accessible by providing aid to students and developing institutions. In 1870, colleges and universities enrolled 50,000 students; by 1960 3.5 million attended—and that figure would double in a decade. The American college was now seen as an inclusive, not exclusive, institution.

As higher education became more accessible, it also became more desirable, and even necessary. No longer a kind of finishing school for the elite, it was now an essential path to employment in many fields. Training for nearly all of the professions took place in colleges and universities, of course. But vocational and technical training was also being offered in the growing number of community colleges which, according to education historian Frederick Rudolph, "were answering an insistent demand for the collegiate experience."[12] Increasingly, the absence of the college degree meant limited opportunity.

This new mood of opportunity through education was also felt in American Indian communities. Perhaps even more than the average soldier, Indian GIs went home with new expectations. Having fought for the nation and experienced life beyond reservation boundaries, they were, according to Indian educator Wayne Stein, "less inclined to endure overt or covert racism, wanted greater freedom from the authoritarian interference of the Bureau of Indian Affairs in their daily lives, and wanted educational opportunities for their children."[13]

But for many American Indian veterans, the transition was especially difficult. There is a whole body of literature describing the personal trauma these veterans faced back home. Despite their hope for a better future, they still experienced blatant racism and limited opportunity. Historian Peter Nabokov writes:

Discrimination was something they fought overseas, but they had forgotten their second-class citizenship at home. In New Mexico and Arizona state law still did not allow Indians to vote. They could not take out GI loans. "Look," a veteran said, "I have a false eye, cheekbone, a silver plate in my head, but I can't buy liquor in a bar like any American."[14]

Termination policies deepened these psychological wounds and revealed the federal government's inability to create a coherent and responsible Indian policy. Although some tribal leaders at first testified in favor of termination, the policy faced uniform opposition as years passed and the consequences became clear. By its conclusion, many American Indian leaders were determined not to be victims again.

But the political, legal, and economic expertise necessary to defend against bad policy and injustice was in short supply. And the emergence of self-determination policies only accentuated the urgent need for an educated leadership. Tribes now set out to get it.

More opportunities for higher education were available through grants and scholarships, and more American Indians were earning college degrees, but numbers remained small after the war and throughout the termination era. In 1957, only about two thousand Indian students enrolled in colleges and universities.[15] Yet the number of college graduates was tiny. In 1961, for example, only sixty-six Indians graduated from a four-year institution.[16] While a growing number of students was enrolling in two-year colleges, and not pursuing a four-year degree, the great disparity in these figures reveals an unnaturally high rate of attrition.

In the postwar years, a number of tribes actively encouraged their members to enroll in college. The Navajo tribal council, for example, sponsored its own scholarship fund in 1957. But they, too, saw disappointing results. Half of the students who went off to college returned home by the end of their freshman year.[17]

## INDIAN CONTROL OF HIGHER EDUCATION

It became clear to Indian leaders and educators that Native American students faced two barriers. First was the struggle to get into college.

Second was the even greater struggle to successfully complete a degree once enrolled. Since the release of the Meriam Report, and especially since the GI Bill and the Higher Education Act, the federal government, as well as individual colleges and universities, had encouraged Indian students to enroll. But as more did, it became clear that access did not guarantee academic success. The dropout rate for American Indians remained at 90 percent or higher at many institutions. Estelle Fuchs and Robert J. Havinghurst estimated 75 percent attrition rate for students who entered a post-secondary institution in 1970.[18]

In this emerging era of self-determination, a growing number of Native American leaders decided to take action. On the Navajo reservation, especially, discussion of a tribally run college first began in the early 1960s. By 1968, with funding provided by the Office of Economic Opportunity, the tribe, and the Donner Foundation, the nation's first tribal college, Navajo Community College, was founded.[19] In turn, other tribal colleges quickly followed in California, North Dakota, and South Dakota. As a model, these tribes turned to America's community colleges. Their philosophy of open admission, job training, and community development closely matched the needs of reservations. According to Wayne Stein, community colleges and their tribal college counterparts have much in common. "Their differences lie in funding sources, jurisdiction, and cultural factors, not educational goals," he wrote.[20]

This does not mean, however, that tribal colleges tried to look and act like mainstream community colleges. Instead, the community college philosophy of local control and dedication to local needs allowed them to become uniquely Indian institutions. Their first loyalty was to the members and culture of their tribal nation, making them institutions of opportunity, not assimilation.

But neither were tribal colleges attempting to exist in isolation from American society. Rather, they sit at the fulcrum between the Indian and non-Indian world, making the western model of higher education accessible and useful to American Indian communities. Graduates leave with both a better understanding of their own cultures and the ability to take part in the larger American society. For the first time, they do not have to make the painful choice between one culture and the other.

Tribal colleges, like their communities, are constantly struggling to find the appropriate balance between the two worlds. Traditions will not be abandoned; indeed, most Native Americans believe they must be nurtured. But most tribal leaders, and most members of the tribal college community, also agree that reservations cannot retreat from the dominant society. Phillip Deloria, then director of the American Indian Law Center, put the challenge this way:

> To refuse, in the name of cultural purity, to learn the skills of survival in the world as it exists is to perpetuate paternalism. It bases continued tribal existence, not on independence, but on the need for non-Indians to maintain a sterile buffer within which Indian culture can be shielded from the real world. All the while the non-Indian protectors continue to make the key decisions.[21]

In this way, tribal colleges have taken Indian societies full circle. From the first years of contact, European educators believed that they could bring opportunity to Native Americans. After centuries of effort, their promises seemed empty. Yet after just thirty years of effort, American Indians have created institutions that do bring educational opportunity—and hope—to their reservations.

# An Overview of Tribal Colleges

L ESS THAN THREE DECADES after the first tribally controlled college was founded, the movement has grown to twenty-seven institutions across the country, and continues to grow. New colleges are still being created and enrollments continue to climb.

Every college is unique, reflecting the culture and economic needs of its reservation. Each has its own distinctive "feel." However, as institutions, the colleges have much in common. Even the newest colleges reflect the vision of the first institutions. They are all organized and funded in similar ways. Likewise, they share many common needs. While there is growing diversity among the colleges, it is still possible to summarize their administration, student body, and financial needs.

## GOVERNANCE

Tribal colleges are, in every case, chartered by one or more tribes and maintain a board of directors that is exclusively or predominately American Indian. Like a state university or public community college, they are formally sanctioned as the institutions of higher learning for their communities.

However, most tribal colleges try to keep an arm's length from their tribal governments, recognizing that administrative autonomy is necessary for both accreditation and their own stability. In some cases, colleges have created ways to insulate themselves from inappropriate interference. Turtle Mountain Community College, for example, has a two-board structure deliberately designed to insulate it from any inappropriate political influence. While the board of directors is responsible for college governance and policies, the board of trustees is responsible for broad

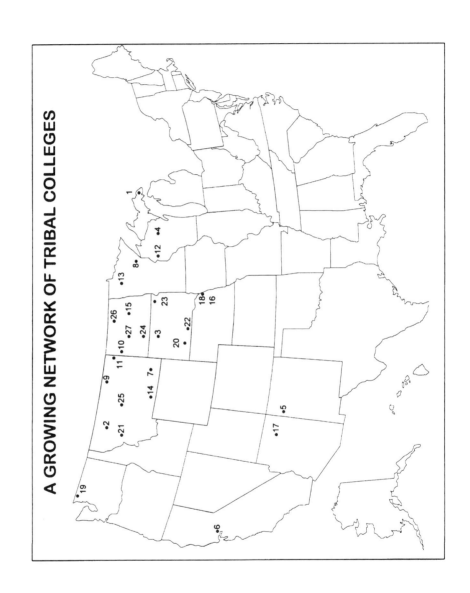

A GROWING NETWORK OF TRIBAL COLLEGES

1. Bay Mills Community College
   Brimley, Michigan

2. Blackfeet Community College
   Browning, Montana

3. Cheyenne River Community College
   Eagle Butte, South Dakota

4. College of the Menominee Nation
   Keshena, Wisconsin

5. Crownpoint Institute of Technology
   Crownpoint, New Mexico

6. D-Q University
   Davis, California*

7. Dull Knife Memorial College
   Lame Deer, Montana

8. Fond du Lac Community College
   Cloquet, Minnesota

9. Fort Belknap College
   Harlem, Montana

10. Fort Berthold Community College
    New Town, North Dakota

11. Fort Peck Community College
    Poplar, Montana

12. Lac Courte Oreilles Ojibwa Community College
    Hayward, Wisconsin

13. Leech Lake Tribal College
    Cass Lake, Minnesota

14. Little Big Horn College
    Crow Agency, Montana

15. Little Hoop Community College
    Fort Totten, North Dakota

16. Little Priest Tribal College
    Winnebago, Nebraska

17. Navajo Community College
    Tsaile, Arizona

18. Nebraska Indian Community College
    Winnebago, Nebraska

19. Northwest Indian College
    Bellingham, Washington

20. Oglala Lakota College
    Kyle, South Dakota

21. Salish Kootenai College
    Pablo, Montana

22. Sinte Gleska University
    Rosebud, South Dakota

23. Sisseton Wahpeton Community College
    Sisseton, South Dakota

24. Sitting Bull College
    Fort Yates, North Dakota

25. Stone Child Community College
    Box Elder, Montana

26. Turtle Mountain Community College
    Belcourt, North Dakota

27. United Tribes Technical College
    Bismarck, North Dakota**

*Not located on a reservation.
**Does not receive funds under the Tribally Controlled Community College Assistance Act; not located on a reservation.

oversight of the college's mission and acts to buffer the college from the tribal council. While college administrators admit that this system appears redundant, they say it works well.[1]

Some colleges have been unable to maintain sufficient autonomy. In a few cases, tribal councils are unwilling to give their college authority to shape and pursue their own policies. Too often at these institutions the president's office is a revolving door and the quality of instruction suffers. This is the exception, however, not the rule. On many reservations, the tribal college is the most stable and most politically independent institution. Even in communities where tribal chairmen come and go with alarming speed, and political scandals, large and small, are a way of life, the college remains strong.

Most college presidents are American Indian and turnover at most colleges is low. Among the twenty-seven tribal colleges, eight are led by presidents who either helped found the institution or were hired soon after it was established. At some colleges, this adds up to ten, fifteen, twenty, or more years of service. Many of the colleges that had rapid turnover in their early years are now able to hold on to their top administrators for five years or more—a very respectable tenure for any institution.

Because the colleges are still so young, and because many administrators started their careers at a young age, even some of the movements "elders" are just now in their forties and fifties. There is, however, a growing concern for the future. Today's presidents are eager to prepare tomorrow's leaders, and to give them the benefit of their experience. Through a Ford Foundation grant, they sponsored a three-year leadership institute for vice presidents, deans, and faculty, offering seminars on the skills needed to run a college. Informal mentoring also occurs at many institutions.

The presidents recognize, too, that the skills needed to start a college are not necessarily the same skills needed to sustain an institution. Founders of the first tribal colleges were deeply committed advocates of social change and many were very effective community organizers. These were valuable skills and allowed the colleges to succeed when the first task was to mobilize support within their reservations and to take their cause to Washington, D.C.

However, many presidents were not trained educators. Most had little or no experience in administration. Over the years, they had to learn through trial and error, and several long-time presidents and other top administrators have returned to higher education to earn doctorate degrees, usually in education. Increasingly, new presidents and administrators arrive with extensive experience in education and the skills needed to maintain budgets, staff, and facilities. The quality of administration, then, is strong and getting stronger.

## CURRICULUM

All tribal colleges began as two-year institutions. The immediate goal was to provide vocational training, especially for jobs available within the reservation. Salish Kootenai College, for example, offered its first courses in forestry, reflecting the importance of the timber industry in the region. Dull Knife College on the Northern Cheyenne Reservation helped train Native Americans to enter the local mining industry. Northwest Indian College, located on Puget Sound, taught aquaculture.

Today, job training still dominates the curriculum, although the range of degrees has greatly expanded. Students may choose from culinary arts and construction trades to human services and tribal management. The most popular degrees, college administrators report, are in the fields of business, health, and education. Most colleges offer one or more certificate or associate degrees in these disciplines, usually in nursing, secretarial science, and early childhood education.

As the colleges grow, more are adding four-year and even graduate degrees. Oglala Lakota College and Sinte Gleska University started the trend. Today, they offer both bachelor's degrees in elementary education and business. Oglala Lakota College offers a master's degree program in tribal management, and Sinte Gleska has a master's program in education. Salish Kootenai recently started a four-year degree in human services. Even many smaller two-year schools are offering students four-year and graduate degrees by working cooperatively with non-Indian colleges and universities. In some cases, the non-Indian institutions send their own faculty to the tribal college to teach classes on site. Increasingly, distance learning technology is being used instead; tribal college students "attend" classes through interactive video.

General education courses add richness to these career-oriented programs, exposing students to the breadth of the liberal arts. This is especially valuable for students who plan to continue their education at non-Indian institutions. Tribal college administrators note that their students often prefer to complete more challenging courses in math, science, and English at a tribal college where more support and encouragement are offered.

Courses in Native American studies are a special part of every tribal college. Indeed, a focus on culture forms the core of the college's mission. All colleges offer courses in their tribe's arts, philosophy, and history. While most students choose to major in career-oriented disciplines, many enroll in one or more cultural courses, and all feel the influence of tribal culture on campus.

## INSTRUCTION

Most instructors at tribal colleges are non-Indian. This is in contrast to the dominance of Native Americans in the administration and student body. Overall, two-thirds of faculty are non-Indian.[2]

However, there is no evidence that non-Indian faculty compromise the mission of tribal colleges or are less respected by students. In The Carnegie Foundation survey of over 1,600 students, only 19 percent said that the larger percentage of Indian faculty was a very important reason to attend a tribal college. In contrast, the higher percentage of American Indian students was very important to nearly twice as many. In addition, the fact that the college was Indian controlled was very important to 41 percent.[3]

Still, college administrators would like to have more Native American faculty. American Indian instructors, it is believed, understand the needs and concerns of their students and, of special importance, act as role models. Their very presence in the classroom offers encouragement and tells students that they can succeed.

Tribal colleges encourage American Indians to apply for teaching positions, but they have a hard time finding applicants. The sad truth is that the supply of qualified Native American faculty is still severely limited. In addition, tribal colleges cannot offer competitive salaries or benefits. Many tribal members with graduate degrees are lured away to better paying positions off the reservation.

Some tribal colleges mentor their own students and other community members, helping them gain the education and experience necessary to return as teachers. Some observers of the tribal college movement believe this mentoring role should be more aggressively pursued, arguing that tribal colleges have an obligation to nurture the next generation of Native scholars. However, most tribal colleges do not have the resources needed to support such a large and long-term project. Informal outreach and encouragement is all most can offer.

Tribal colleges do reserve a special place for tribal members as instructors of culture, language, and traditional philosophy courses. In most cases, only members of the tribe hold this essential knowledge. Many of these traditional scholars are elders with little formal education. They come into the classroom certified by the college as experts in their field and often hold a place of honor on the faculty. Tribal elders also serve as formal and informal advisors to the college, especially on cultural issues.

The high faculty turnover rate may be the greatest concern for college administrators. While tribal colleges attract instructors who are sensitive and dedicated, they have a hard time finding people who will stay. One survey of tribal college faculty found that 60 percent of instructors have been teaching at the institution for just five years or less.[4] Again, poor pay and harder living conditions conspire to push faculty away. This lack of continuity requires colleges to expend a great deal of energy on recruitment and faculty orientation. It may also slow the growth and maturing of academic programs.

However, all instructors—both Indian and non-Indian, new and old—are praised by their students. Indeed, the high regard held for teachers was an especially significant finding in The Carnegie Foundation survey. Overall, 69 percent of the students surveyed were very satisfied with the teaching at their college. Only 1.9 percent were somewhat or very dissatisfied. In each case, they felt their instructors were knowledgeable, accessible, and enthusiastic. For example, 68 percent strongly agreed that their professors enjoyed teaching, and 70 percent strongly agreed that the professors encouraged students to participate actively in classroom discussions.

In addition, they believed instruction at their college was superior to instruction at non-Indian colleges. Thirty-six percent of respondents said they had previously attended a non-Indian college or university. Of those, 88 percent agreed that tribal college faculty are friendlier, and 93 percent agreed that more individual attention is shown to students at a tribal college. Finally, 72 percent agreed that the quality of instruction was higher at their tribal college.

In written comments, students again chose to focus on the dedication of the instructors, and all staff. When asked to summarize their college's greatest strength, many gave responses similar to this one: "The professors enjoy teaching and know each student by name. They are always willing to answer any question any student has. The staff seems to care about improving the college for the benefit of the students." Another summed it up with a word: "Encouragement!"

Colleges have no greater responsibility than to bring students into a community of learning and engage them actively. When students feel that they are more than names on a class roster, and know that their ideas will be treated with respect, then they become scholars, not just bodies sitting in desks. They know, too, that personal effort will be rewarded, and their absence will not go unnoticed. In this role, tribal colleges not only succeed, they excel.

They succeed, in part, because they are small institutions and it is almost impossible for a student to get lost in the crowd. But it is also true that tribal colleges have a dedication to students that most other colleges and universities cannot match. In all that the colleges do, their first priority is to support students and ensure their success.

## Students

Total enrollment among all tribal colleges continues to climb rapidly. In 1989, the college reported a total enrollment of over 10,000. In 1995 this number doubled to over 20,000.[5] Among the colleges, student enrollments vary greatly. In most cases, this reflects the age of the institution and the size of the community it serves. Navajo Community College remains the largest, with a total enrollment estimated to be 1,500. Total enrollment at other tribal colleges may be four hundred or less.

Clearly, the total number of students is low compared to the number of non-Indians in higher education. Indeed, all tribal college students combined add up to the equivalent of just one state university campus. However, many of the reservations with tribal colleges have as few as three thousand members. In these communities, the impact of even a dozen students with college degrees is significant. And because every tribal college takes on a wide range of community development programs, their work either directly or indirectly enriches the lives of nearly every tribal member. In contrast, the federal government has poured millions of dollars into some reservations through programs that, all too often, had far less positive impact than the tribal colleges.

From the beginning of the tribal college movement, most students were older and most were women. The typical tribal college student was often described as a single mother in her early thirties. Tribal college officials explain that this population was the least served by higher education, yet was the most eager to get a degree. Women with children, especially, are often determined to get off welfare and provide for their families, but are unable or unwilling to leave home and attend schools in distant cities. For them, tribal colleges were the only option.

Today, the average age of students has dropped slightly as more students in the traditional eighteen to twenty-one age group enroll. At Turtle Mountain Community College, President Gerald "Carty" Monette called this a "second wave" of students. They have not replaced the older student body, but their numbers are growing.[6]

In The Carnegie Foundation survey, the average age of respondents was twenty-seven, suggesting a slight drop in age, assuming the earlier anecdotal evidence was accurate. But at a few colleges, the change may be even more dramatic. At Salish Kootenai College, for example, administrators were taken by surprise during fall 1994 class registration. It seemed every new student was eighteen, nineteen, or twenty—a full ten years younger than the average student. Even a quick stroll through that institution's campus confirms the trend. Ten years ago, it was hard to find a young student. Today younger students can be found chatting in the student lounge, sitting in groups outside on warm days, and cramming for tests in the library.

Some colleges say there is also a more even male/female ratio. However, approximately 70 percent of the Carnegie survey respondents were women.

The shifting demographics is subtle but is evidence of change, and suggests that even greater changes will soon take place. It first reveals that tribal colleges are accepted as legitimate institutions of higher learning in their communities. Many high school graduates at first shunned the tribal college down the street, believing it was not a "real" college. The younger student body suggests that it may now be seen as a college of first choice—not just last chance—by more tribal members.

In addition, some colleges are attracting students from outside their communities. While a few institutions, such as United Tribes Technical College and D-Q University, are deliberately intertribal, most of the colleges were created to serve a specific reservation. All still see this as their primary mission, but as reputations grow and a wider variety of degree programs are offered, students are arriving from both neighboring and distant reservations.

## FACILITIES

Nowhere is the evidence of the tribal colleges' creativity—and need—more immediately apparent than in their facilities. The buildings that make up a typical tribal college campus are too often a hodgepodge of rented storefronts, trailers, and leftover buildings. Classroom and office space is usually severely restricted and many lack adequate space for student lounges, dining facilities, gyms, and other "extras" that most college students in America take for granted.

In the early days of the college movement, students and administrators took pride in their willingness to park a double-wide trailer in a field and declare their college open for business. And many demonstrated great creativity in their search for space and equipment. Today, like all pioneers, they tell stories of their early days with humor and some nostalgia.

Sinte Gleska used a once-abandoned federal building that had no heat or electricity. Wobbly desks were propped up with legs made from soda cans. President Lionel Bordeaux recalls that the college's sole typewriter was missing the letters "r" and "y." Space was so tight that classes were held in hallways.

Salish Kootenai's first home was the second floor of a rented building in the reservation town of Ronan. There, librarian Bob Bigart fought a slow-motion battle for space against the administration. President Joseph McDonald recalls that Bigart secretly tried to expand the college's nascent library by pushing his bookshelves beyond their allotted space an inch or two every night. He hoped other staff would not notice that he was slowly encroaching on their cubicles.

Almost every college has stories like these, told to laughter at community gatherings. But such depravation quickly grows old. The struggle to meet even basic needs lost its romantic appeal long ago. Today, many are resigned to working under conditions most staff, faculty, and students at non-Indian colleges would simply find intolerable.

Little Big Horn College, for example, has been celebrated for its innovative campus. There, the main building is a renovated gym. Offices are in one set of former locker rooms, classrooms are in another. We learned during our first visit ten years ago that the former shower room had just been converted into a biology lab. The basketball court–sized gym was being converted into a library. Meanwhile, a sewage treatment plant a half-mile away was turned into a science laboratory. Students would squeeze past a large steel tank on a narrow metal catwalk to have class in a small room to one side.

More typical is the campus of Turtle Mountain Community College.

There classes are held in a series of simple buildings constructed as money became available. With a creative administration, the facilities are adequate, but President Carty Monette admits they are not elegant. As at most colleges, the struggle is to supply enough space for the bare necessities.

Some colleges have been able to find the resources needed to build a true college campus. Navajo Community College took advantage of federal funding in the 1970s to build a campus complete with a cafeteria, recreation facilities, and student housing at its main center in Tsaile, Arizona. One of the newest colleges, Fond du Lac Tribal and Community College, is housed in a stunning new building that features tree trunks for columns and curving glass walls.

Salish Kootenai College, meanwhile, has patiently built a very attractive campus amid a pine forest in Montana's Mission Valley. Several buildings are built partially underground and one is solar heated; on cold days a single wood-burning stove warms much of the building. Other buildings were built by students from the building trades program. All are attractive and thoughtfully designed.

But even these colleges are cramped for space. New construction barely keeps up with growing enrollments, and even the best-equipped colleges usually lack adequate space for students. In addition, sufficient materials for learning, from computers and library books to lab equipment and desks, are often in short supply.

Staff and faculty are painfully aware of these limitations, but students responding to The Carnegie Foundation survey were especially blunt in their appraisal of their college's facilities. When asked to describe the greatest need of their institution, the majority of students talked about the shortage of space and equipment. Some simply said they needed a bigger campus. Others described specific deficiencies. "Dining facility, a larger place to study, a bigger library," said one. "More classroom space and classrooms," said another. The wish list continued: computers, dormitories, gym, more books and periodicals, a student lounge. For some, the needs were elemental: some requested such basics as desks, chairs, and bathrooms. One asked for "heat."

When asked to rate specific facilities—such as study space or lab equipment—students were less critical. For example, nearly 50 percent said their access to computers was excellent. But in contrast to the lavish praise from students for their institutions in other areas, most responses about facilities were clustered in the "good" to "fair" range.

Student responses and campus tours confirm that most colleges are able to meet the basic needs of students, staff, and faculty, and some excel. But at most colleges, students, staff, and faculty all see the evidence of need every time they walk into a classroom, office, or library.

## Funding

The greatest challenge to all tribal colleges is the persistent search for funding. While the movement, as a whole, will certainly survive, each college's ability to grow and better serve its community is contingent on support from outside of reservation boundaries.

Tribal colleges must look beyond their borders, in most cases, because their own communities are too poor and they do not have wealthy alumni able to contribute. In addition, tuition, which averaged $1,580 per year in 1994–95, is already slightly higher than most two-year colleges and cannot be increased significantly without pushing away students. Instead, they survive on a collection of grants, gifts, and federal appropriations that, too often, adds up to little more than a starvation diet.

Financial support provided by the federal government is especially vital. Navajo Community College benefited from federal aid in its early years and today receives approximately $7 million annually. In addition, most of the other colleges owe their very existence to the Tribally Controlled Community College Assistance Act of 1978 and its annual appropriation that has now grown to over $19 million.[7] This funding, first sought by the colleges in 1972, is critical for each of the tribal colleges.

The available funds are distributed according to each college's Indian student count; no money is distributed for non-Indian students. Only Navajo Community College is funded according to need rather than enrollment, but support to that institution has fluctuated over the years.

The importance of this legislation cannot be overstated. For most tribal colleges, it is essential for survival. Indeed, during the 1996 budget impasse, when government programs were only partially funded through a series of continuing resolutions, the impact on tribal colleges was almost immediate. When payments did not arrive from the Bureau of Indian Affairs, tribal colleges were required to cut back staff and, in some cases, take out loans to make payroll. Few colleges had the resources needed to fill even this temporary loss of funding.

College leaders are, however, more worried about funding over the long term. They note that government support is still not keeping up with the growth in tribal college enrollment. Although the total amount appropriated has climbed—indeed, it has more than doubled in ten years—it has not kept pace with the colleges' growing enrollments. Congress first authorized $4,000 per student in the original legislation, a figure later increased to $5,820. But the amount actually released has never matched this figure. In 1996, funding per student was $2,900, or just half the amount authorized.[8] Increased appropriation is a priority for the colleges.

Some tribal colleges also support their institutions through federal grants that fund vocational education. Of special importance, tribal colleges were recently designated as Land Grant colleges, which offers both direct annual payments from an endowment and opportunity to take part in a wide range of programs in the Department of Agriculture.

Foundation support is also critical. In our first report, we noted that few philanthropies were reaching out to tribal colleges. Within the past ten years, however, significant support has come from both regional and national foundations, including US West, MacArthur, Pew, Ford, and others. Most recently, the Kellogg Foundation has launched a $22 million initiative in Indian education, much of it targeted at tribal colleges. Additionally, the Lannan Foundation has developed an Indigenous Communities Program that also offers significant support to the tribal colleges. Although these programs cannot replace essential federal funding, they do allow colleges to develop programs that directly benefit students and their communities.

## Working Together

All of the nation's tribally controlled colleges are members of the American Indian Higher Education Consortium. The organization was first formed in 1972 by six of the oldest tribal colleges, allowing the movement's leaders to share information and, of special importance, help gain federal support. Today, all colleges receiving funds through the Tribally Controlled Community College Assistance Act are members. There is a small number of Indian-controlled colleges not affiliated with the consortium, but most are young institutions that have not yet approached, or been accepted into, the group.

The consortium also includes three government-supported institutions of higher learning: Haskell Indian Nations University, Southwest Indian Polytechnic Institute, and the Institute of American Indian Arts. In addition, one Canadian college—Red Crow College—participates in consortium meetings. These institutions share many of the same goals and hold a similar philosophy of education.

The consortium for most of its recent history had no central office and supported no staff. Instead, all AIHEC business was conducted by presidents and staff from member colleges. The organization's tiny budget, collected from dues, did allow the colleges to hire a part-time consultant who monitored federal legislation and presented testimony to Congress.

However, the consortium has grown in recent years. Increased dues and several grants have allowed the colleges to purchase an office in Alexandria, Virginia, and pay for a professional staff of five. This office is now playing a vital role by managing grants, offering support to colleges, and gathering data on the needs and accomplishments of the colleges.

The consortium also sponsors a quarterly publication, *Tribal College: Journal of American Indian Higher Education*. This editorially independent publication is currently located in Colorado with a staff of two. Articles and research document the work of the colleges, helping administrators and faculty share information with colleagues within and beyond the tribal college movement.

In 1989, the colleges created another organization—the American Indian College Fund. Located in Denver, with additional offices in New York, its mission is to raise money from foundations, corporations, and individuals. Money is used to build an endowment and support student scholarships. Although less than ten years old, it has enjoyed great success and some presidents hope it will play an even more important role in the future.

# CHAPTER IV

# Tribal Colleges in Context

ALMOST FROM THE MOMENT of first contact, the demise of American Indians has been predicted. Missionaries, educators, soldiers, and federal bureaucrats have, for centuries, created policies around the assumption that Native American cultures—and even Indians as a people—were doomed. They were nearly correct. Disease, alcohol, relocation, military conflict, and the active suppression of culture did great harm. From the arrival of Christopher Columbus to 1900, the Indian population declined from an estimated high of 5 million or more in what is now the United States to less than 250,000.[1]

By the early nineteenth century, the deathwatch had begun. Painter George Catlin traveled by steamship up the Missouri in 1830 to capture on canvas a people he was convinced would soon no longer exist in flesh. "My heart bleeds for the fate that awaits the remainder of their unlucky race," he mused.[2] He and others also collected artifacts, and even physical remains, as proof of their existence.

But 160 years later, Western historian Patricia Limerick dryly observed the obvious: "Indians survived their much predicted death."[3] Today, five hundred years after Columbus, Native Americans continue to exist as a distinct people. The population has grown to over 1.5 million. And despite attempts to eliminate reservations and force assimilation, long-held values and traditions remain.

Indians are not going away. Indeed, Native American culture is resurgent. While acknowledging that Indian society cannot retreat from the non-Indian culture, Native Americans are recapturing and celebrating values that have sustained them for generations. Many tribal leaders and community activists are convinced that answers must come from within their own communities. Reservations do have a future, they say, if their members are willing to acknowledge problems, draw on their own strengths, and devise their own solutions.

Reflecting the attitude throughout much of Indian Country, one influential tribal member of the Crow Nation in Montana put the issue pointedly during our first visit in 1988: "We cannot rely on the Bureau of Indian Affairs to run our future for us. We cannot rely upon the people of Billings and we certainly cannot rely upon the state of Montana for self-government. We have to rely upon ourselves for self-government. If we can do that, I believe we have taken many steps back in time when the Crows were a great nation."

Tribal colleges are an essential part of this change. But they are also part of a larger effort by Native Americans to rebuild reservation societies and take control of their own future. For their work to be understood, it is therefore necessary to place them in context of the communities they serve. In this chapter, we examine some of the key issues facing reservations, and look at some of the innovative solutions being devised by Native Americans to build a stronger future.

## ECONOMIC EMPOWERMENT

Decade after decade—through each era of reform—reservation poverty has been a fact of life.

In the nineteenth century, commentators both sympathetic and critical inevitably remarked on the "squalor" they saw on newly created reservations. Placed on inhospitable tracts of land, Indian wards were offered substandard food and routinely cheated by corrupt officials. "Today they . . . subsist on rations doled out to them with a niggardly hand by government agents," confirmed Captain J. Lee Humfreville in 1887.[4]

During World War II and immediately after the Indian New Deal, *Look* magazine paused from its war coverage to print a photo of a small boy standing in front of his home on the Navajo Reservation. The caption reads: "This Navajo child, little more than a baby, stands barefooted and virtually naked on a snow-covered reservation in Arizona—his need as dire as that of any child in war torn Europe."[5]

In 1969, in the heart of the Civil Rights movement, the Citizens Advocate Center, in a scathing report on the status of Native communities, found that on the Pine Ridge Reservation unemployment reached 60 percent and the median income was just $1,910. At the same time, it noted that $8,040 was spent each year per family by the federal government to eliminate poverty.[6]

How are reservations faring today? Unemployment varies widely, but on Pine Ridge and many other reservations it still reaches as high as 60 percent, or higher, according to tribal leaders. Shannan County, South Dakota—which encompasses the Pine Ridge Reservation—is repeatedly called the poorest county in America. In 1989, the average income for Indians living on reservations was $4,478.[7]

Most reservation economies are stagnant; the few existing jobs mainly lie in the public sector. "Federal and tribal governments, schools, and the U.S. Public Health Service are the major employers in most tribal communities," said Schuyler Houser, a tribal college administrator who has studied tribal economic needs.[8] And because there are few reservation-based businesses—such as grocery stores, pharmacies, and other essential services—the money that is generated invariably flows like water off the reservation and into non-Indian pockets.

It is tempting, then, to say that little has improved for Indians in the past century, but this implies that change is impossible and that reservations are communities without a future. Fortunately, there are other, more hopeful stories to tell:

- On the Turtle Mountain Reservation, a fully tribally owned data entry company, UniBand, Inc., now employs eight hundred people and has contracts with the federal government and major corporations. In recent years, the company has also established itself at thirteen sites across the country, including Virginia, Florida, and Texas. According to the Turtle Mountain College President Carty Monette, UniBand now generates about $36 million per year—most of which is reinvested in the company for future growth.[9]
- On the Rosebud Reservation, the Sicangu Enterprise Center has for over ten years helped tribal members start or expand

small, home-based businesses through a "circle banking" program first developed in Bangladesh. The peer lending program helps tribal entrepreneurs who do not qualify for traditional bank loans. In recent years, the center has helped people make and market traditional quilts, buy tools for automotive repair, and set up a fireworks stand, among many other enterprises.[10] Although income is usually supplemental, one study found that 87 percent of tribal members engage in some kind of micro-enterprise.[11]

• Meanwhile, the Crow Reservation is taking advantage of its location adjacent to Little Big Horn Battlefield. Although the site of Custer's last stand is a popular tourist stop in the West, the tribe has benefited little from the station wagons, minivans, and motor homes that pass through. But the recently established Institute for Microbusiness and Tourism now offers Indian-designed and led tours of the site, as well as fly-fishing trips on the Big Horn River and historic tours of various reservation sites.[12]

Mainstream press accounts routinely focus on the legacy of poverty and government neglect, but when tribal leaders and community activists are asked about economic issues, many prefer to talk, instead, about evidence of change. Although these and many similar programs have yet to transform most reservation economies, their importance should not be underestimated. All reflect an important new approach to economic development.

They demonstrate, first, a determination by tribes to take charge of their economies. In the past, nearly all economic development initiatives were devised and—in many cases—fully managed by the federal government and non-Indian groups. Yet nearly all failed to bring lasting change and many left reservations only more devastated. Allotment—the break-up of reservations into small farm-sized parcels in the late nineteenth century—and termination policies in the 1950s were, in part, responses to Indian poverty, but produced only more. Tribes, aware of this history, know that solutions cannot be imposed by the federal government.

They also prove that reservations are not economic blank slates. Although poor, many do support a stable network of small, home-based microenterprises and, with it, a true entrepreneurial spirit. This economy is invisible to most non-Indians. But, increasingly, it is viewed as an important asset by many tribal leaders and, especially, community-based organizations who treat it as a foundation for future growth.

For example, Cheryl Crazy Bull, director of development at the Sicangu Enterprise Center, explained her organization, first started to support microenterprises, is now looking for ways to help the growing number of small businesses, reflecting new-found economic sophistication in the community. "A lot of people who are working in microenterprise organizations are leaving to start their own businesses because they gained the insights," she said. "More people are getting educated about business development."

This kind of microenterprise and small business development is a priority across Indian Country. Revolving loan funds are running on the Pine Ridge Reservation, the Crow Reservation[13] and elsewhere. Meanwhile, on the Turtle Mountain Reservation, a local business association supports the approximately two hundred small businesses now established in the community.[14]

Finally, and of special importance, examples of success help disprove the long-held assumption that economic development is incompatible with native cultures. Non-Indian policymakers have for centuries argued that tribal values were an impediment to economic progress. Communal land and a lack of "ambition" struck many as especially backward. U.S. Senator Henry Dawes revealed a great deal about both the native and Western world view when he chastised the Five Civilized Tribes in 1887 for lacking "selfishness" which, he contended, "is at the bottom of civilization."[15]

In contrast, tribal economic development often celebrates traditional culture. This is, of course, expressed in the products and services some businesses provide—from traditional pottery to cultural history tours.

But at a deeper level, these values are expressed in how businesses large and small are run, and the role they play in their communities.

Jerry Reynolds, a staff member at First Nations Development Institute in Virginia, says many tribal economic programs reflect a more "holistic" view of economic development where the goal is not simply wealth but community development. In this way, business growth becomes part of a larger agenda for social renewal, encompassing issues as diverse as housing, the environment, cultural renewal and political sovereignty. "For example, the whole notion of entrepreneurialism is different," Reynolds said. "You are not an individual entrepreneur on the Donald Trump model. You are a person who knows how to do a few things that benefit the *whole community*, and yourself in the process."[16]

First Nations Development Institute has nurtured this approach since 1980 by supporting, through grants and technical assistance, a variety of innovative economic development programs. It helped establish the nation's first microenterprise lending circle on the Pine Ridge Reservation, for example, and now supports the Sicangu Enterprise Center on the Rosebud Reservation.[17] Among many other projects, the institute also supports an ecotourism program on the Ft. Belknap Reservation of Montana that is helping rebuild cultural pride on the reservation.

These are tangible signs of progress, and demonstrate how much has changed in recent years. Schuyler Houser noted the trend: "A generation of problem-solvers who have the necessary confidence and the skills [are beginning] to address these issues, as big as they may be. They may not have magic wands, but they may be able to change the local situations, if only incrementally."[18]

However, even some of the most enthusiastic supporters of tribal economic development acknowledge that significant barriers remain. Houser and others stressed that, despite some progress, key ingredients for economic renewal are still missing in most communities. Stephen Cornell, summarizing tribal economic development in his book *Return of the Native*, ticked off a daunting list of obstacles:

> Few reservations have the natural resources of such tribes as the Navajos, Utes, Jicarilla Apaches, and others; many are isolated

from markets, transportation networks, and centers of population; skilled workers are rare. Outside investment is key, but not easy to find.[19]

There is, then, no economic "magic bullet." And even some of the most exciting new approaches have limitations. Fort Peck College President James Shanley, for example, stressed that while small business development is the hot trend, it alone cannot build healthy economies. Small and isolated reservations can support only a limited number of services, he argued. At a certain point new enterprises only split the limited pool of reservation money.[20]

Instead, he believed a broad-based economy, based on business, manufacturing, agriculture and more is necessary. His assessment is confirmed by Stephen Cornell: "The trick will be to develop diversified economies that are neither corporate appendages nor hostages to the whims of a single market. The successes so far are few."[21] These hurdles are also shared by many rural communities nationwide, as well as poor inner-city neighborhoods.

It is important to note, then, that self-determination does not mean an end to outside support. Neither do early signs of economic success imply that private giving is no longer needed. Instead, poverty dominates most Indian communities.

Unfortunately, tribes are finding it harder to make their case. Even as data continue to show Native Americans to be, as a group, among the poorest in the nation, there is growing misperception that Indians no longer need support. The remarkable rise in tribally run casinos, especially, has created false images of wealth that threaten to reduce funding from both government agencies and foundations.

A handful of tribal groups have, indeed, struck gold. The tiny Mashantucket Pequot tribe of Connecticut, for example, has built what may be the largest casino in the western hemisphere, located near several major cities and lacking nearby competition. Thousands of gamblers arrive daily at Foxwoods Casino, bringing money to the tribe and its approximately three hundred members.

Unfortunately, this highly publicized success story may give the impression that all reservations do, or can, generate similar wealth.

Unlike the Pequots, however, most tribes are located in rural and poor communities. Their casinos will never bring in the same number of visitors with deep pockets. Also unlike the Pequots, most tribes have significantly higher enrollments and a broader range of social needs. The revenue their casinos do generate becomes only a valuable supplement, not a cure-all.

In addition, for every tribe that has a casino, four do not. Some are opposed to gaming. The Navajo Tribe—the nation's largest—voted not to have casinos on their reservation.[22] Others have not been able to negotiate a satisfactory gaming compact with their state—a federal requirement. It is also important to note that tribes without casinos do not receive any money from those that do, just as the gaming or lottery revenue generated by one state is not shared with another.

Finally, casinos face an uncertain future. Gaming is on the rise across the nation. Some observers believe that as competition increases, fewer gamblers will travel additional miles to reservation-based casinos.

## CULTURE: REBUILDING TRADITIONS

Reservations do not conform to popular images of the Wild West. Today, most "Pintos" and "Broncos" are cars, and tribal members dress more like cowboys than Indians. Nearly all residents live in government-built frame houses, not traditional shelters, and those not on welfare may work as secretaries, lawyers, nurses, teachers, construction workers, or government administrators.

This is confusing to many tourists. "Every summer we get hundreds of people on the reservation and they are really disappointed because I don't have my feathers on, I don't ride my spotted horse, I don't live in a teepee," said Albert White Hat, an instructor at the Sinte Gleska University on the Rosebud Reservation and nationally known spiritual leader. "Some visitors literally walk past us because they didn't see those things."

At the same time, many Native Americans and non-Indian scholars also talk about how much has changed: Many speak with great sadness about the loss or—perhaps more poignant—the impending loss of an ancestral language. In some communities, the number of fluent speakers can be counted on a single hand. They describe, too, the loss of their own history, once carefully passed from generation to generation through the oral tradition. These stories of the elders are, in a very real way, the archives of a nation.

But it is equally important to highlight how much has not been lost, how much has been successfully rebuilt and, especially, how this knowledge is helping tribes build a stronger future. Although traditional lifestyles are no longer lived—no teepees, no wigwams, no feathered natives on horseback—long-held values remain part of the fabric of daily life.

Continued White Hat: "We're trying to bring a positive image back. We're telling the young people that they can be proud of who they are and what they are. They don't necessarily have to wear a feather to be an Indian, but what is inside—how they look at themselves—is what's important. You know, traditions can be carried on whether you wear blue jeans or traditional costumes."

On some reservations, the expression of culture is obvious to even casual observers. Driving through the Navajo Reservation, car radios pick up a station where DJ's alternate effortlessly between English and Navajo. On the Crow Reservation nearly all tribal members are skilled in their own language, and about 87 percent of adults speak it as their first language. There, traditional spiritual ceremonies, while not universally practiced, remain fully integrated in the society. Traditional sweat lodges sit in the backyards of many otherwise American-style reservation homes.

The arts, too, remain a vibrant expression of culture. Indeed, for many non-Indians, pottery, rugs, beadwork, and silver jewelry—often based on centuries-old traditions—are their most tangible connection to Native Americans. Some Pueblo pottery created today uses design patterns that archaeological evidence proves are thousands of years old.[23]

Less obvious to outsiders is how long-held values continue to shape not just clay, but also relationships, community values, and a larger world view. Uniquely tribal notions based on kinship, respect for elders, connections to the land, and more still carry great weight, even on reservations that appear transformed by the outside world.

On the Flathead Indian Reservation of western Montana, for example, the reservation's border is distinguishable only by a small sign as Route 93 rises over hills before dropping dramatically into the Mission Valley. Inattentive drivers on this busy road—popular with tourists heading north to Glacier National Park—might not know they had stumbled into a piece of Indian Country. Dominated by non-Indian businesses, the route is lined with convenience stores, tourist stops, boutiques and drive-through espresso stands.

But here the cultures of the now confederated Salish and Kootenai tribes have survived and, according to many members, are growing stronger. Tribal languages are once again formally taught; the tribal council recently funded language schools for children age three to five where Salish and Kootenai are taught in an immersion program, for example.[24] And respect for traditional spiritual practices—once kept alive by a dwindling number of spiritual leaders—is being embraced by younger generations, say community members.

This revival dates back to the mid-1970s when the Salish and Kootenai tribes each formed their own Cultural Committees. Worried that old values were not being carried on and angered by what they saw as the insensitivity of white anthropologists, the tribes started their own programs to record and promote tribal culture. With their own buildings and trained staff, projects focus on the recording of oral histories, stories, and traditional beliefs of tribal elders for local distribution. Cultural events are also held and courses in traditional arts provided to students and the community.

When we first visited the Salish Cultural Committee's Longhouse in 1988—a thoroughly modern building in the town of St. Ignacious— director Clarence Woodcock was helping a group of local women and students learn how to make teepees. The large, sunny room was filled with bolts of canvas and the sound of sewing machines. He spoke about the rebirth of traditions. "When I was growing up, the feeling was that it wasn't good to be Indian," he said. "This has changed."

Important, too, is the renewed influence of tribal elders. Both cultural committees now sponsor monthly meetings of elders who—

reflecting their traditional role as leaders—advise the tribal council and tribal organizations. They are also consulted before new logging or construction begins to ensure that burial and spiritual sites are not disturbed. They hold no office, but their opinions often shape tribal policies. "They're informal but they have a very important role," explained Joseph McDonald, president of Salish Kootenai College.

On a recent autumn morning the Salish elders gathered to hear a presentation by two members of the tribe's natural resources office. Handouts covered the tables as staff described proposed changes to the tribe's hunting and trapping regulations. Already drafted by the department, it was open for public comment before a council vote.

Although the changes were relatively minor, the presentation generated a lively discussion. Of special concern was a proposal to prohibit fishing licenses to children younger than eleven. Several elders recalled how fishing was an important part of their own childhood and were not happy with the restriction.

Tribal staff said they were concerned about injuries and resulting liability, but their audience was unmoved. Echoing complaints heard throughout America, one member said the tribal government was taking over a role once reserved for parents. Others focused on cultural issues. "Let's not take the right of the kids to grow up and learn what they need to learn," said Pat Pierre.

"So should we take the reg. out?" a staff member finally asked. Well, at least lower the age limit, another elder proposed. And so the cordial, low-key conversation continued until the meeting broke for a buffet lunch served on paper plates.

Native American culture is not—and never has been—stagnant. From the beginning of European arrival American Indians have been adapting and changing, selecting what was useful and, within their power, discarding what was not. The gathering of elders that day—treated by participants as a normal and unremarkable part of tribal life—stands as quiet testimony to the tribe's ability to adapt, but also to keep what is theirs.

In turn, the same spirit of cultural renewal is felt on reservations across the country. Tribes are working conscientiously to teach traditional skills and values to their children, and even reshape whole institutions to more fully reflect tribal values. For example, on the Pine Ridge and, more recently, Rosebud reservations of South Dakota, community leaders have proposed the creation of an entirely new form of tribal government. Some argue that the tribal council system, imposed through the Indian Reorganization Act of 1934 and modeled directly after the federal system, does not reflect traditional emphasis on consensus and shared responsibility. Community forums are held to discuss alternative approaches.

Although new and not yet tested, these proposals show how the active expression of culture is growing stronger and more confident. Further, it reveals how culture is not "holding Indians back," but is being used as a tool to build stronger societies and help members participate more fully in American society. Culture—in all its forms of expression—is alive and well.

## HEALTH AND WELLNESS: HEALING COMMUNITIES

Health care is a concern on every reservation, where data continue to show that Indian communities still suffer disproportionately from a daunting list of ailments.

Important progress is being made. Indeed, by some measurements, the battle for primary health care is slowly being won. Infant mortality has declined dramatically, for example. More than twice the national average in 1955, it is now actually lower than the national average, according to 1985 data. Likewise, maternal deaths have also dropped. Overall life expectancy continues to trail the white population, but the gap narrows with each passing decade.[25]

But, without question, significant needs remain. Many isolated reservations are not served by a hospital or clinic. In addition, cultural differences and a legacy of distrust still divide Native Americans and Western medicine. A 1991 study by the American Indian Health Care Association found that cultural misunderstanding and bureaucratic barriers were especially troublesome.[26] Non-Indian medical professionals, it found, too often failed to understand the medical needs of Indians.

Here, too, there is evidence of change. On the Navajo Reservation, medicine men are welcome in the Indian Health Service Hospitals and one hospital has even constructed a "healing room," designed in the shape of a traditional hogan. In maternity wards, meanwhile, the smell of burning cedar is common—smudging with smoke is often used during labor.[27]

In addition, the number of Native American doctors and nurses, while still disproportionately small, is growing. Between 1980 and 1990, the census reported 868 American Indian physicians—a 63 percent jump—and 7,524 registered nurses, a 92 percent increase. Special credit goes to the University of North Dakota which, for over twenty years, has supported an innovative program called Indians Into Medicine (INMED). By reserving ten of its sixty medical school entry slots for Native American students, this one school has graduated one-fifth of the nation's Indian physicians.[28]

Increasingly, reservations are also taking responsibility for alcohol and drug abuse by tribal members which, according to many tribal leaders, remains the top community health issue. Leaders on some of the reservations we visited said alcoholism rates reach to 80 percent. A tribal college counselor on the Standing Rock Reservation of North Dakota estimated it was 90 percent in that community.

Not surprisingly, disproportionately high rates of accidental death, alcohol-related liver disease, and domestic violence result, leaving no family untouched by its impact. Michael Dorris's 1989 book, *Broken Cord*, meanwhile, made the whole nation aware of Fetal Alcohol Syndrome and its impact on children and, through them, the future of Native communities.

For many years, alcoholism was not openly discussed. Believing little could be done, tribal members did not speak against drinking and many communities had no alcohol education or treatment programs. Even where programs did exist, their work was not always supported by tribal leaders.[29]

However, the mood has changed. Reservation leaders now report that alcoholism is being acknowledged and, within the past decade especially, sobriety has reached the level of a crusade. Many Indian organizations have declared their events alcohol-free and reservations sponsor "sobriety walks"—marches and rallies that focus on public awareness. On Pine Ridge Reservation, a recently established chapter of MADD—Mothers Against Drunk Driving—has petitioned the tribal council to more aggressively enforce laws against bootlegging and drug dealing.[30] As tangible evidence of progress, treatment centers often have waiting lists and, according to nationwide data, the number of alcohol-related deaths is slowly dropping.

These programs reflect, in part, a larger battle against substance abuse in the United States. But it is also a reflection of tribal cultures. Community activists link the movement to the rebirth of traditional spirituality and cultural recovery, arguing that one cannot exist without the other.

As a model, they look to Alkali Lake, a small Native community in Canada. There, alcoholism was so rampant that, it was said, not a single adult was sober many Saturday nights. But in 1972 one couple gave up drinking, triggering a movement that has resulted in 98 percent sobriety in the community. Their story was told in a 1987 film that, while not well known in the non-Indian community, was widely circulated in Indian Country.

IN EACH AREA—economic development, cultural survival, and community health—there is evidence of progress. Certainly, much work remains. What we describe here are only the hopeful stirrings of a movement. But without question, the climate has changed.

Tribal colleges helped shape this movement. In many communities, they were the first to address economic, cultural, and social issues. And, today, they continue to devise programs that address these and other needs. In the following chapters we look at the role of tribal colleges and their impact on the lives of students and, especially, whole reservation communities.

# CHAPTER V

# *Fulfilling the Vision*

TRIBAL COLLEGES ARE PART of a movement for fundamental social change within reservations. Their mission is to rebuild cultures and, in the end, create new and stronger nations. Explained Sinte Gleska President Lionel Bordeaux during our first visit: "We're yet in our infancy but because of the potential that we possess, people look to us as the hope of the future, the vehicle to the future."

Native American educator Jack Forbes made the argument forcefully in the early years of the tribal college movement:

> Native tribal and folk groups especially need their own institutions in order not merely to preserve that portion of their heritage which proves to be worthy of preservation, but also in order to develop sufficiently a degree of self-confidence, pride, and optimism . . . A Native American university can serve as an agency for helping to restore the quite obvious ability in self-management and self-realization which Indians possessed prior to the intervention of the federal government.[1]

To succeed, tribal colleges had to overcome significant barriers. But to a remarkable degree this vision has been sustained and after three decades real progress is being made. Tribal colleges have had a measurable impact on their students and have helped start and lead a movement for social and cultural renewal. As experience and resources grow, their reach extends even deeper into the culture and farther into the community.

In this chapter we feature the work of the colleges and describe how they serve students, strengthen communities, and rebuild cultures. We describe the kinds of programs they offer and examine evidence of their success. But we also try to convey at least a little of their spirit and creative energy, which is also vital to their success.

## SUPPORTING STUDENTS

First, tribal colleges offer access to higher education. As an essential foundation, most colleges are located on reservations and, in the tradition of public community colleges, all are open admission, welcoming anyone with a high school degree.

For those who have not completed high school, the colleges typically offer tutoring for the high school equivalency exam, also known as the GED. Indeed, The Carnegie Foundation survey found that 20 percent of students first completed the GED before enrolling at the tribal college. At some schools, the percentage is even higher. At Lac Courte Oreilles Ojibwa College, for example, approximately one-third of the student body earned a GED through its own tutoring and testing center, said President Jasjit Minhas.[2] Likewise, Turtle Mountain College reports that 34 percent of its students arrive with a GED.[3]

The colleges also confront other, more subtle, barriers to enrollment. Within reservations, the greatest obstacle is often psychological—the belief that higher education is something foreign and intimidating. Tribal college staff work especially hard to eliminate fears in ways that are often simple but still effective.

At Blackfeet Community College in northwestern Montana President Carol Murray talked about the importance of college-sponsored meals, called "community feeds." These events—where as many as five hundred tribal members might attend—are significant on a reservation where poverty is pervasive. But they also create an important bridge into the community. "Incomes are so low, we have to feed them," Murray asserted. "But we also want them to feel comfortable here. . . . We want to build collegiality among all adults on the reservation."

Many tribal colleges also allow their campuses to be used as community centers, where all tribal members—not just enrolled students—regularly gather for meetings, celebrations, and cultural presentations.

Indeed, during one of our early visits to Little Big Horn College, President Janine Pease Pretty-On-Top stressed the value of this community service. In her reservation, she told us, the college was the only politically neutral space available to all.

The significance of this accessibility should not be overlooked. For decades American educators fretted over the high dropout rate of Indian students. Yet this tragedy did not reveal how completely American higher education failed to serve Indian communities: For every Native American student who entered college, many others never made it to the front door. Physical distance, poor academic preparation, and a lack of confidence existed as obvious but unsolved barriers. Simply by making college available—geographically, educationally, and emotionally—to all who could benefit, tribal colleges rearranged the landscape of Indian higher education.

But access is not enough; support must continue after enrollment. Because tribal colleges are nonselective, they are required to serve even those who are academically unprepared and more easily sidetracked by family responsibilities and a lack of money. Because an estimated 85 percent of tribal college students live below the poverty level—and all live in poor communities—simple problems become difficult hurdles for many students. A student may drop out because a car breaks and there is no money for repair. Another leaves because baby-sitting is lost. Too many others come with even more profound needs; counselors say alcoholism, drug abuse, and domestic violence are prevalent.

Tribal colleges try to respond to the special needs of each student. Some offer transportation for those without cars, and daycare centers for those with small children. Alcohol and substance abuse counseling may be available. In every case, tribal college staff understand the needs of students and are sympathetic to their concerns.

Personal attention also makes a difference. Because tribal colleges are small, staff and faculty are able to work together and address the needs of each student. "Academic advising, financial aid counseling, and career-planning assistance can often be interwoven for each student by faculty and staff who are familiar both with the individual and with the institution's processes," said Schuyler Houser.[4] And when a student's needs cannot be met on campus, referrals are made to other nearby community-based social service or counseling programs.

Placement testing is usually mandatory for incoming students; when weaknesses are found, students are placed with tutors or in basic skills classes. Reflecting a trend nationwide, tribal college administrators say math and English skills are especially weak. Lac Courte Oreilles Ojibwa College President Jasjit Minhas said his institution's placement tests routinely discover students reading at the third- or fourth-grade level. Frequently, students will spend a full academic year building essential college-level skills before beginning their coursework. Overall, he said, nearly one half of all students need at least some tutoring.

Many tribal colleges offer counseling services. In addition, "College Life" classes help students make the transition to higher education by discussing everything from note-taking strategies to time management. Because most tribal college students are the first in their families to go to college, these and other essential skills must be formally taught.

The importance of college cost and financial aid must be acknowledged. Tuition and fees average $1,580 during the 1994–95 school year. This is about the same as the typical public two-year college, and well below the $2,686 spent by students at the average public four-year college. It is far below the cost of private two-year and four-year institutions. Further, because most tribal colleges cater to commuter students, room and board costs are eliminated.

There is a false perception among many Americans that Indians get a "free ride" through college. Although the federal government and individual tribes do offer grants and loans for Indians, these programs are inadequately funded and serve only a small percentage of eligible students. Instead, most Indians, like all Americans, rely on traditional financial aid packages, usually built around Pell Grants and college Work Study.[5] And because formulas for funding these programs favor older colleges, tribal college students receive a disproportionately small share of even these funds.

The reality is that most students struggle to make ends meet. The typical student has little savings and cannot rely on family members for aid. Instead, most students are themselves parents who attend college while also taking care of children or other family members.

These students require special understanding and support from the colleges they attend. Explained Salish Kootenai College President Joseph McDonald: "We're always having to figure out some innovative way to get them money. Sometimes we just write them a check. Maybe they had to attend a funeral, but don't have money for the bus home. Or they can't pay their rent and are about to be evicted."

His and other tribal colleges also offer scholarship money raised by the American Indian College Fund. Tuition and fees may be waived for students who do not qualify for Pell Grants or for other reasons. In 1996, McDonald said his institution waived $600,000 in tuition money—a significant sacrifice for his college.

## THE INFLUENCE OF CULTURE

For decades, educators understood that the transition to college was, for many Native American students, an especially disorienting experience. Even when students arrived academically prepared and financially secure, success was not guaranteed. Separated from home, they were confronted with unfamiliar values and expectations. Researcher Danielle Sanders reported, for example, that much of what Indians find in non-Indian educational institutions "runs contrary to the social norms, self-perceptions, and expected behaviors that they have learned at home and that have been reinforced in their own cultural community."[6] Even those who persisted in college often talk about the inferiority and isolation they felt.

In contrast, tribal colleges eliminate this discontinuity between the college and community. Within each classroom and across the campus unique values are celebrated, not challenged, and special needs are understood, not ridiculed. Rather than being a disorienting experience for Indian students, college represents a reinforcement of values inherent in the tribal community.

Their work begins in the classroom where students, perhaps for the first time, are encouraged to learn about their own heritage. On the Lummi reservation of western Washington State, Northwest Indian

College offers classes in Indian knitting, spinning, beadwork, drumming, and the carving of masks, totems, and canoes. Nebraska Indian College teaches quilt making, silverwork, ribbonwork, bustle making and shawl making. Fort Belknap College in North Dakota includes hide tanning and porcupine quillwork. Navajo Community College teaches rug weaving among its many courses. Lac Courte Oreilles Ojibwa Community College teaches classes in Native American song and dance, storytelling, traditional healing practices, and ethnobotany.

What is the value of these courses? They, of course, keep traditional skills alive—helping students create objects of beauty or sustain spiritual practices. But teachers and administrators stress that the arts and philosophy, once dismissed as Indian "crafts" and "superstitions," represent much more. They help build a sense of pride and unity necessary for the health of any community.

Gerald Slater, vice president of Salish Kootenai College, helped us appreciate the importance of these courses during our first visit. "Many young people have a history of heavy drinking and have, in general, a lack of self-respect," he explained. "But as they get more involved in traditional culture, they begin to get new self-respect. Sometimes they will quit their drinking and begin to find a life that is more meaningful for them."

He continued: "Forced assimilation has resulted in a lack of respect for Indians and their ways. Now people are realizing that these ways are good. They're different, but there is nothing wrong with them. There is a sense of pride and dignity that comes with it."

That evening, Myrna Chief Stick, a part-time instructor at the college, sat alone in an empty hallway while her class prepared for its final exam in Coyote stories. An important part of many Indian societies, Coyote stories are used to explain natural events and offer, at the same time, essential moral lessons. Students had spent the semester discussing these tales and were getting ready to act out one such story for Chief Stick.

While waiting for her students to call her back into the classroom, she too spoke of the "self-respect, dignity, and honesty" that traditional culture provides. "Through the work of the tribe and the college," Chief

Stick said, "tribal members are starting to identify these values for themselves. In the last four or five years, people are becoming more aware than they have been in years."

The six students in the class, talking after their presentation, offered similar ideas. Wallace Shorty asserted that classes in traditional culture and language offer students insight into their own identity. "A lot of kids are Indian, but they don't know what it means to be Indian," he said. "They don't know how to go about it."

Classes in Native American culture also ensure that traditional knowledge will survive. Relocation, allotment, boarding schools, and the forced suppression of cultural expression disrupted the traditional flow of knowledge from parent to child. Tribal colleges put lost knowledge back into the hands of the younger generation. Another student explained: "A lot of our elders and a lot of our people who told these stories are now dead. Their children and grandchildren don't know them. I'd like to be able to pass them down."

But tribal colleges try to do more than preserve the past. The modern expression of arts and contemporary literature is also featured. For example, at the Fine Arts Institute at Sinte Gleska University, students are urged to explore new ways of expression through sculpture, painting, and photography. Modern Native American contributions to literature— including the poetry of N. Scott Momeday, and the novels of Leslie Marmon Silko and Louise Erdrich—are on the reading lists of classes at many colleges.

Tribal history, law, politics, and social issues are another unique dimension of the tribal college curriculum. Few non-Indian colleges even try to explore the full complexity of contemporary reservation societies. Even fewer do so from a Native American perspective. Yet, nearly every college offers courses that explore the history and modern concerns of their own tribe.

Oglala Lakota College has a three-course sequence in Lakota history, and others in Lakota culture and social systems. Dull Knife College has a course in the "Role of Native American Women." D-Q University, an intertribal college in California, examines the complexity of federal Indian law and tribal legal systems.

Although most students choose not to major in Native American studies, cultural courses are popular and, in the classes we observed, the quality of instruction is high. Visiting a small campus center run by Oglala Lakota College in the town of Martin, South Dakota, we listened to a class discussion of Chief Crazy Horse. Conversation was lively and intense as students compared family stories with history texts. On the adjacent Rosebud Reservation, a course in Lakota spirituality at Sinte Gleska University felt more like a graduate-level seminar as students examined how sophisticated concepts had been misinterpreted by non-Indian scholars. At Salish Kootenai College, every seat was filled for a class on tribal history. On that day, the instructor talked about development of the region's fur trade, describing how American Indians learned to successfully participate in the Western economic system.

It is important to note that these courses represent only one part of the curriculum. All tribal colleges also feature the kinds of classes recognizable to any college student in America: math, science, English composition, and American history. Degrees—from welding to elementary education—have requirements similar to any other community or four-year college. Elective courses range from step aerobics to earth science.

However, the influence of tribal culture is not limited to a specific list of classes or a separate Native studies department. Instead, the impact of culture is felt across the whole campus and in nearly every class. At tribal colleges, culture is more than a subject to be taught. It fully shapes each institution and its philosophy of education. Many tribal colleges work deliberately to include Native American perspectives in every class. When we first visited campuses in 1988, this represented a new movement, and we observed how innovative faculty were finding approaches to teaching that helped Indian students succeed. Some were working to insert an Indian viewpoint even in distinctly Western courses, such as math and science. Other teachers made classes more "culturally appropriate" not by changing the content but by changing how the subject was taught.

At Little Big Horn College on the Crow Reservation we spent a day with Bob Madsen, a creative and enthusiastic science teacher who was finding ways to build student interest and reduce anxiety. Most tests were open-book he told us and could be repeated if the grade was too low. "I don't put a weight around their necks," he said. "If they get a D, they take the test over until they do A work." This encourages success, he said, but also reflected the value placed on forgiveness in the Crow culture.

He also stressed the relevance of his subject to students. "A big part of what goes on in the class is not determining the composition of calcium, but learning to solve problems," he said. "The math and the science are there, but it is tied to concrete things." He said, however, that the focus on success does not mean that academic quality is lost. "I love to give out As, but I make them earn them. This is a place where good science can happen. It is not just at Montana State University or Harvard that good science is possible."

At Turtle Mountain College, we visited with math instructor Sister Margaret Pfeifer. She believed students are best able to succeed when the air of academic competition is replaced by greater cooperation, a philosophy appropriate for a community that stresses family obligations over individual advancement. Her math assignments frequently allowed— even encouraged—group work and mutual assistance. As a result, she told us the quality of the classwork goes up along with retention rates, while anxiety over this traditionally stressful discipline goes down.

In the last ten years this philosophy has grown and matured. Tribal culture is even more confidently expressed not just in classrooms but across campus. Increasingly, college leaders are taking the next step by working to make their colleges even more responsive of tribal values. Some are eager not only to add elements of native thought and philosophy but also to make their colleges as fully reflective of their cultures as most other colleges are of western culture.

Navajo Community College has worked especially hard to build the college on a foundation of tribal culture. This search was first reflected symbolically: Its main campus is located at the geographic center of the reservation and design of its six-story, glass administration building is inspired by the hogan.

But within the past decade, college leaders have also worked to shape a distinctly Navajo philosophy of education and, in the process, started to remold the college and the curriculum. The goal, says president

Tommy Lewis, is not to adapt a Western philosophy of education, but to start from scratch with a model of education that is fully Navajo. "Rather than having education come at us from the outside, education has to start from within," he argued. "Rather than try to copy people, we just reached deep inside our teaching and found out that all the answers to education are there." At this college, every class is expected to reflect a Navajo perspective.

For example, a recent class in Navajo Astronomy combined western concepts with Navajo knowledge, freely mixing the insights of Harvard University physicists and Navajo elders. Taught as a science course, it included observations of the night sky and a field trip to Hansen Planetarium in Salt Lake City. But the approach to learning was strictly Navajo. The class was organized around the traditional Navajo calendar; sacred stories were told at the proper time of year, and the Navajo language was incorporated. No textbooks were used. Instead, students were encouraged to conduct research by talking with elders. "In many respects this personal research went beyond anything previously published," the instructors reported.[7]

Salish Kootenai College, meanwhile, is finding new ways to teach the culture of its tribe. In an experimental program, some students are learning not in the classroom or through formal instruction but by working directly with an elder in the community. This duplicates the traditional role of elders who taught their knowledge informally and over time.

Another approach is found at Oglala Lakota College, where former instructor Tom Allen developed the graduate-level "Manager as Warrior" curriculum. In an effort to reconcile the discipline of business management with traditional values, Allen identified seven key Lakota values and matched them with the values of the modern business world. For example, the traditional value placed on bravery correlates the business need to be proactive, an attribute identified by Stephen Covey in the *Seven Habits of Highly Effective People*. Meanwhile, the value placed on generosity correlated with Peter Drucker's admonition to "focus on your contribution."

Allen was not attempting to artificially twist Lakota culture to meet the needs of the modern business world. Rather, he is showing that the qualities inherent in his culture already allow for success; there is no need to "sell out." This, he says, dispels the belief that American Indian values "are contradictory to being a productive citizen or good manager."

This project is another example of how the colleges are working not just to embed culture in the curriculum but to create new models that are unique hybrids of old and new, Native and Western. This is the kind of work tribal colleges are uniquely qualified to undertake. They are committed to their cultures, yet they understand that students want tangible rewards. Therefore they offer culture as a tool of opportunity, not simply as an interesting academic subject.

Students confirm the value of this Indian-centered environment. Ninety-five percent of those who responded to The Carnegie Foundation survey agreed that "American Indian values and customs are respected at this college." Over 85 percent agreed that Indian values were felt in most of their classes. And, significantly, 87 percent agreed that they felt comfortable at the college "because it reflects the values of American Indians."

In these ways, tribal colleges are building institutions that are uniquely Native American. Their vision is clear and, to us, compelling. But what of the results? Are tribal colleges succeeding?

Comprehensive data on student outcomes have not been adequately compiled. Although tribal college enrollment has grown significantly, too little is known about student persistence after enrollment. This, in part, reflects the difficulty of assessment, especially at community colleges where students enroll for many different reasons. For example, tribal college administrators point out that while many students arrive hoping to earn a degree, others enroll in classes only for personal enjoyment or to build job-related skills. In The Carnegie Foundation survey of currently enrolled students, for example, 10 percent said they were taking classes but were not pursuing a degree.

Additionally, a significant number of students "stop-out" before eventually earning a degree. Indeed, in our student survey, 24 percent reported that they had previously attended a tribal college. A few of these students had completed a degree and were returning to earn another. But most had left before finishing their program. When asked why they left, the most frequently cited reasons were money and family responsibilities. Now they were back again, ready to continue their education.

Turtle Mountain College President Carty Monette argued that many of these students are experimenting with higher education by repeatedly leaving and returning, testing their interest and ability to succeed before fully committing themselves. "We're still educating about what higher education is, what the value is," he said.[8]

Graduation rates are affected by the kinds of programs a college offers. Vocational degrees and certificates tend to have higher completion rates since they often lead directly to employment. Many job-training programs may be completed in a few months or less and have close to 100 percent completion rates. Students move immediately from the classroom to employment in a tribally run casino, industry, or office. Overall graduation rates tend to be lower, however. Although no reliable studies have been conducted, several long-time presidents estimated that between one-quarter and one-third of students who enter leave at some point with a certificate or degree. If this is true, then tribal colleges have graduation rates comparable to public community colleges nationwide.

While data on retention and graduation are still missing, there is growing evidence that persistence is rewarded. Recent surveys of tribal college graduates consistently find that most are employed or continuing their education. Their success is all the more striking when compared to the poverty and unemployment that exist in most reservations.

The most comprehensive study was conducted by Carty Monette. His research, based on a survey of over five hundred graduates of Turtle Mountain College from 1980 to 1990, found that most were working or continuing their education. Less than 13 percent reported they were unemployed, which, noted Monette, "is in sharp contrast to the total rate of unemployment among Indian people nationally and among Turtle Mountain Chippewa in particular."[9] Further, the majority of graduates continue to live on or near the reservation—indicating that the college's academic program matched local employment opportunities.

Monette also found that 56 percent of graduates continued their education at a non-Indian college or university and, among this group,

32 percent had earned a four-year degree. He noted that these figures *exceed* the transfer and graduation rates of community college students nationwide. Tribal college leaders have long argued that students who first enroll at a tribal college were more likely to succeed when they transferred to a non-Indian institution than students who went directly to non-Indian colleges. The data from this one institution supports that assertion.

Other colleges have also tracked the progress of graduates and found similar evidence of success. Fort Belknap College reported that between 1992 and 1996, 122 students completed degrees and 46 transferred to other colleges and universities. In addition, 200 students found employment after completing one or more classes, and of that number 133 found employment in a field related to their training.[10]

Meanwhile, Crownpoint Institute of Technology reported that 85 percent of graduates are employed. The figure is 87 percent at Little Big Horn College[11] and 93 percent at Oglala Lakota College.[12] On the reservations these colleges serve, meanwhile, unemployment exceeds 60 percent.

These employment numbers for graduates, while impressive, do not reveal the full impact of tribal colleges in their communities. Since most graduates stay on the reservation, they are able to share their knowledge and new skills with the entire community, and serve as role models. Most colleges, for example, offer business degrees that allow graduates to work in government offices and, it is hoped, build local economies. Health care is also a growing profession. Several colleges offer two-year nursing degrees that help increase the number of Indians in this important profession.

Education degrees are increasingly popular. Both Sinte Gleska University and Oglala Lakota College have their own four-year degree programs in elementary education, and Sinte Gleska offers a master's degree in the field. Many other tribal college are now offering education degrees through distance learning or two-plus-two degree programs with non-Indian institutions. The goal is to increase the number of Native American teachers committed to meeting the needs of Indian children. On some reservations their impact is already felt: At one elementary school on the Pine Ridge Reservation, twenty-one of twenty-six teachers are graduates of Oglala Lakota College.[13]

## SERVING COMMUNITIES

All tribal college leaders believe they also have a responsibility to reach out to the surrounding reservation and offer a wide range of essential services. From literacy tutoring to small business development, tribal colleges are full-service centers for community development. Although many tribal colleges now offer four-year and even graduate degrees, they are all, in the truest sense, community colleges, where the focus is on social and economic advancement for all members.

Many colleges offer cultural programs to the entire community. Blackfeet Community College has a traditional encampment each year for school children. Bay Mills Community College runs a summer language institute where Ojibwa is reintroduced.

Leech Lake Tribal College, meanwhile, has developed an innovative community gardening project that encourages tribal members to improve their health by growing indigenous beans, corn, squash, and other traditional foods. Called Project Grow, the goal is to improve diets and, especially, reduce the incidence of diabetes, while also building respect for tribal traditions and traditional spirituality. Currently, 250 gardens are being cultivated and, says academic dean John Morrow, their impact is felt across the reservation. "It's a holistic approach," says Morrow. "We use our language, reconnect with the earth."

Tribal colleges also work to provide vital social services through housing, alcohol counseling, job training, and more. Blackfeet College President Carol Murray, for example, forged a partnership with an alcohol treatment center on her reservation. The project began after a recent visit to the house where residents were living. "If you thought our campus was bad, you should see this place. It was worse," she said. Special plastic sheeting was used to cover portions of the dilapidated, leaky roof.

The college agreed to offer classes in reading, math, and other academic areas, but residents were also taught carpentry skills by working to repair their own home. Through this one modest program, the college

provided better housing and taught an employable skill. Some participants have since gone on to complete a degree from the college, and one
remarkable student has completed a bachelor's degree from a state
university.

In another project, Little Hoop Community College is running an
innovative child development center that also focuses on the needs of
parents. The Comprehensive Child Development Center offers child care
and health screening for infants, toddlers, and young children.[14] But staff
also help parents continue their education, find jobs and, if necessary,
overcome alcohol and substance abuse. The college has been responsible
for the tribe's Head Start program since 1985; currently it serves one
hundred children. But this new, expanded program has special value in
a reservation community, according to former president Merril Berg. By
paying attention to the needs of whole families—even grandparents and
other relatives—the college is recognizing that the needs of children are
inseparably linked to the needs of whole communities.

Tribal colleges also reach out to tribal members through the media.
Salish Kootenai College runs its own television station and produces a
variety of shows of special concern to tribal members—including forums
with candidates in tribal elections and reports on the tribe's forest
management.[15] Meanwhile, Fort Berthold College has developed its own
radio station. Similarly, college libraries become a community resource.
Frequently, they are the only libraries on a reservation. Academic titles are
typically supplemented by general interest books and even children's
literature.

Economic development is a priority for every tribal college. Administrators recognize that it is not enough to teach job skills. On
reservations where few jobs exist, tribal colleges must also help nurture
economic opportunity. Within the past several years, a number of colleges
have created small business development centers and made entrepreneurship a priority.

Typical is the Business Assistance Center at Northwest Indian
College, where community members get help developing business plans,
filling out loan applications, and managing their business finances. In
1994, the director of this program established a similar center at Salish

Kootenai College; within weeks of opening, her appointment book was filled with the names of community members eager to open new businesses or expand existing enterprises.

More recently, Fort Belknap College established its own Small Business Development Center. During its first year, the center has sponsored entrepreneurship classes and helped participants develop business plans and complete loan applications. Staff are also working with local artists, helping them learn how to price and market their products.

In a community where unemployment hovers between 65 and 70 percent and few Indian-owned businesses are operating, business skills are severely limited, said director Caroline Brown. For aspiring entrepreneurs, the center must emphasize the basics: "There is a great need to develop knowledge of what is expected of an entrepreneur," she said. "It's not only putting in the time, but also the business side: accounting and record-keeping, the importance of paying bills—and the importance of collecting on your bills."

Other colleges take different approaches to economic development. Turtle Mountain College, for example, is planning to include a small business "incubator" on its new campus. This center will offer low-cost office space to tribal entrepreneurs and encourage collaboration with students and faculty. Tribal colleges have also actively participated in the creation of microenterprise loan funds now running on several reservations, including the Lakota Fund on the Pine Ridge Reservation and the Sicangu Enterprise Center on the Rosebud Reservation.

Finally, tribal colleges serve communities by supporting tribally based scholarship. Several colleges maintain tribal archives and are collecting records and historical documents that, too often, were kept only in distant research libraries. Staff from Oglala Lakota College's archives have systematically collected family histories, gathering data from Indian census roles, allotment documents, and even historical photos held in the basement of the Smithsonian's Museum of Natural History. Blackfeet Community College, meanwhile, has recorded and transcribed oral histories from tribal elders.

This work reflects a long-standing frustration within many reservation communities that too much of the research conducted by non-Indians is inaccurate and inaccessible. Salish tribal elder Jonny Arlee put the complaint succinctly:

> Non-Indian researchers have come into our communities in the past and have only scratched the surface of our Culture and have gained enough knowledge to help themselves in earning their Degrees and use this material for their own gain. Then, when the younger Tribal members who are seeking special knowledge ask for assistance from these Non-Indian researchers, they are discouraged by the fact that these Outside Researchers are asking for a price, or there [are] copyrights to the material, and other obstacles.[16]

The most recent trend in tribal college scholarship is to examine how research is conducted. Believing that the Western view of research, based on the scientific model, cannot adequately answer all of the questions Native Americans ask, some are attempting to develop a new research model. Informally, tribal college faculty and other Native American scholars are working to legitimize traditional scholarship, which often emphasizes values taboo in the Western academic world, such as the oral transmission of information, spirituality, and community control.

Tribal colleges are responding to the immediate needs of their communities through economic development, social services, and cultural awareness. But they are also taking the next step by systematically studying the needs of their communities and proposing solutions that are practical and appropriate.

# CHAPTER VI

# Recommendations for Action

I N OUR FIRST report we applauded tribal colleges for their vision and early evidence of success. But we also stressed that they could not reach their full potential without additional support from both the public and private sectors. We said:

> The goal must be to assure that by the year 2000, the network of community-based tribal colleges created by Native Americans, colleges that offer quality education to their students and bring a spirit of renewal to their nations, is funded, expanded, and flourishing.

We concluded with ten recommendations for action, urging greater support to these young and struggling institutions. Now, on the eve of the twenty-first century, we return to these original recommendations and look for evidence of progress. Has the nation reached out to the tribal colleges? Have the colleges taken full advantage of the opportunities provided? Are they, in fact, "funded, expanded, and flourishing?"

Now is an appropriate time for reassessment. Although the movement is no longer new and untested, the colleges are still poorly funded and dependent on outside support to meet even day-to-day operating expenses. Their ability to grow and mature is largely determined by forces they cannot control—federal budget policies and, more broadly, the nation's attitude toward American Indians.

Our first report on tribal colleges coincided with a renewed interest in Indians, one of America's cyclical "rediscoveries" that seem to come approximately every twenty years. Indian-theme movies—from *Dances with Wolves* to Disney's *Pocahontas*—became a distinct genre for a few years and Indian issues were regularly featured in national magazines, newspapers, and on network television.

But these eras quickly end. Tribal colleges, which found a sympathetic audience ten years ago, now worry about retrenchment and cutbacks. Funding levels rose in the early 1990s, but are now again failing to keep pace with student enrollment. Although the colleges have enjoyed several important legislative successes since our last study, they are still funded at levels below most other institutions of higher learning.

More broadly, we worry, too, about a changing attitude in America toward Native Americans. The very things that capture the nation's imagination—their distinct cultures, the evidence of profound social need, their unique status in the nation's legal and political systems—also frustrate us when conflicts develop and simple solutions are not found. Romantic attachment is too often followed by disillusionment and disinterest.

The needs of Native Americans and their communities do not disappear when the spotlight is turned elsewhere. Now, as strongly as ever, we repeat our conviction that tribal colleges deserve continued support from the nation. Their value has been proven, but their vision is not yet fulfilled.

◄○►

*First, we once again urgently recommend that the federal government adequately support tribal colleges by providing the full funding authorized by Congress for the Tribally Controlled Community College Assistance Act. Specifically, we recommend that the $5,820 authorized per student be appropriated and that, from this point on, federal appropriations keep pace with the growth of Indian student enrollment.*

The Tribally Controlled Community College Assistance Act of 1978 provides essential support to Indian colleges. The funds released through the act were, in fact, critical for the establishment of many of the tribal colleges. And without this legislation many, and perhaps most, of the nations tribal colleges would have to close.

Early tribal college leaders worked hard for passage of this modest legislation. Their ability to work together, master the political process, and overcome frustrating setbacks has become the stuff of legend within the tribal college community. With justification, their success is treated as a watershed event in the history of the young movement.

Twenty years later, however, the full benefit of this Act has yet to be felt. In the original legislation Congress authorized $4,000 for each full-time equivalent student at tribal colleges, and raised it to $5,820 in 1986, but the amount appropriated has never matched those figures. Although the total appropriation has increased, funding has consistently failed to keep pace with the even faster rise in student enrollments. Indeed, at the time of our first report, funding *per student* had dropped to a dismal $1,900!

The early 1990s saw increased support; funding per student reached $3,178 by 1994—the highest level ever achieved. Considering that this was also a period of growth for the colleges, the increased funding was especially significant and we applaud the commitment of Congressional members and staff who became strong advocates for these little institutions.

But even in that year, appropriations were only slightly more than half the level authorized. And now we are again watching a decline in per student funding, dropping to $2,900 in 1995, and threatening to go lower in a climate of federal budget-cutting. Yet the diminished support is even more significant when figures are adjusted for inflation. In constant 1981 dollars this was the equivalent of a mere $1,785. In their testimony before Congress, American Indian Higher Education Consortium staff also noted that authorized funding should have risen to $8,450 to keep pace with inflation. In other words, the funding gap is still large, and growing.

For tribal colleges, the federal government remains their only consistent source of financial support and the Tribally Controlled Community College Assistance Act is their lifeline. We once again urge Congress not to penalize the colleges for their success. Full funding must be the first goal.

Recently passed federal welfare reform legislation makes this recommendation even more timely. As services to the poor and unemployed are

APPROPRIATIONS FOR TRIBAL COLLEGES UNDER
THE TRIBALLY CONTROLLED COMMUNITY COLLEGE ASSISTANCE ACT OF 1978
*(Title I, P.L. 95-471)*

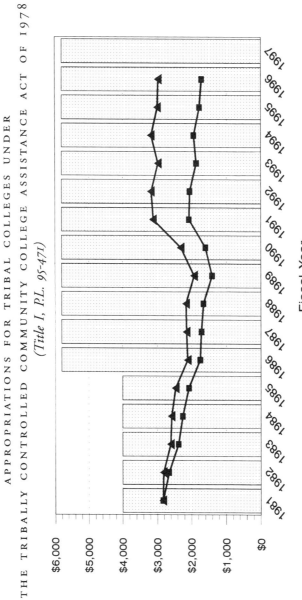

Fiscal Year

☐ Amount authorized by law

◆ Amount actually appropriated, current year, operating dollars per full-time Indian student

■ Amount actually appropriated, operating dollars per full-time Indian student, adjusted for inflation

SOURCES: American Indian Higher Education Consortium.
Current year appropriations taken from BIA reports.
Inflation calculated from Consumer Price Index, Bureau of Labor Statistics.

cut back and shifted to the states, administrators say a greater burden will be placed on tribal colleges. Several presidents explained that they will have to offer even more support services—such as housing, day care, and transportation—to accommodate unemployed students who, in certain states, will no longer be eligible for benefits. Lac Courte Oreilles College President Jasjit Minhas estimates that one-third of his students are directly affected by the sweeping changes. He and others are likewise concerned that tribes will receive a disproportionately small share of the state welfare block grants; states have shown reluctance to pass funds on to these communities which, from the perspective of state legislators, are federal responsibilities.

At the same time, we remain concerned about the relationship between the Bureau of Indian Affairs and tribal colleges. The BIA is the agency responsible for requesting tribal college funds in each year's budget and distributing the money in a timely and efficient manner directly to the schools. In this way, the Bureau is expected to be both a partner and advocate for the institutions.

In reality, it has been a relationship too often marked by mistrust and tension. Tribal college administrators noted that Bureau staff actually testified against funding of tribal colleges in the movement's early years and have in the past also failed to establish regulations required by the legislation. In the 1986 reauthorization hearings, for example, Senator Mark Hatfield, then chairman of the Select Committee on Indian Affairs, reported that the BIA had "failed to establish regulations, or even to publish proposed regulations for comment" on amendments voted on three years earlier.[1]

At the time of our first report, some tribal college presidents saw this as a form of political sabotage. "The BIA refuses to acknowledge, fully and sincerely, our existence," charged Sinte Gleska University President Lionel Bordeaux.

Has anything changed? "Yes and no," said Carty Monette, president of Turtle Mountain College. "They've stopped requesting cuts for us [in the final budget requests]. On the other hand, they haven't requested any increases for us. We continue to be at level funding which, in reality, is a decrease when all things are considered."

We applaud any evidence of progress. However, we remain concerned that the BIA has not yet become a strong advocate for the colleges. These institutions should be viewed not as a regulatory burden, but as a crucial link between the government and the reservation communities they serve, and as a resource that complements and extends the BIA's own programs. Support for these colleges, therefore, helps fulfill the Bureau's responsibility to promote Indian welfare and development.

It is important to emphasize that tribal colleges also look beyond the BIA for support. Most tribal colleges have, at least periodically, received funding through the Carl D. Perkins Vocational Education Act. Indeed, two colleges—United Tribes Technical College and Crownpoint Institute of Technology—are funded primarily through this program. In addition, tribal colleges have in the past routinely participated in Title III of the Higher Education Act, Aid for Institutional Development. Additionally, discretionary grants have also been awarded by agencies such as the Department of Defense, Department of Housing and Urban Development, and the U.S. Forest Service.

However, tribal colleges are often at a disadvantage when they compete for these grants. Many departments and agencies do not know tribal colleges even exist. In addition, many federal programs—even those specifically designed to benefit minority institutions—often inadvertently exclude tribal colleges.

"For example," explained a position paper prepared by the tribal colleges, "a federal agency may offer grants to benefit four-year minority nursing programs, but tribal colleges will be ineligible because they are primarily two-year institutions." Or, it continued, grants for research will be awarded only to institutions awarding doctoral degrees, presumably unaware that, while tribal colleges do not offer Ph.D.'s, many have made research a formal part of their mission statements.[2]

Tribal college leaders hope that a recently signed "Executive Order" will help correct this imbalance. This document, signed by President Clinton in the fall of 1996, directs all federal agencies to examine their programs and find ways to assist the colleges and build effective partnerships.

Although an executive order does not directly allocate money, it does give the colleges the visibility they need. For the historically black and Hispanic colleges—each with executive orders of their own—it has brought greater participation in federally funded programs. Tribal colleges hope to gain equity in funding through their own executive order. We urge that this executive order be conscientiously implemented.

For the federal government, then, our recommendation has three parts. First, we believe the tribal colleges deserve full funding through the Tribally Controlled Community College Assistance Act. Second, the Bureau of Indian Affairs must become an advocate for the tribal colleges, looking after their financial needs as aggressively as they defend their own institutions and programs. Finally, we believe the government's trust responsibility must be acknowledged by all federal agencies. Through the tribal colleges' executive order, the colleges will be able to participate equally in the programs and services federal agencies offer.

◄○►

*Second, we strongly urge full appropriation of Land Grant funds. In addition, we call on state Land Grant colleges to support the work of tribal colleges.*

In 1994, the tribal college leaders won another significant legislative victory when Congress designated their colleges as Land Grant institutions. The original Land Grant Act of 1862 helped establish institutions of higher learning in every state dedicated to the teaching of "agriculture and the mechanic arts." Acknowledging that tribal colleges play a similar role within their reservations, Congress added them to the venerable list of colleges and universities.

The original Land Grant colleges were funded through the sale of federal land or land scrip. Tribal colleges, in lieu of land, were given an endowment of $4.6 million which grows by an additional $4.6 million each year. Interest payments are distributed equitably to each college.

Each college also receives an annual payment of $50,000. Additional funds have been authorized for agricultural extension, facilities, and equipment.

However, the impact of Land Grant designation extends far beyond these dollar figures. Tribal college leaders note that land represents a tribe's one significant, and permanent, resource. The Navajo Reservation alone is the size of West Virginia. But while its spiritual significance is strong, its economic potential has not been fully developed by tribes. Federal, state, and county programs in agriculture, meanwhile, too often bypass reservations and Indian farmers. Tribal colleges hope that, as Land Grant colleges, they will have greater opportunity to develop appropriate agriculture and forestry programs. Some look forward to programs that respond to unique economic barriers and distinctive cultural values. For example, they may help bring traditional foods back into cultivation and develop more environmentally sensitive farming and land use techniques.

Tribal college leaders are still exploring the potential opportunities this legislation creates, but are eager to take full advantage of the programs and services the act now makes available. As a first step, we urge senior Land Grant colleges and universities to support tribal colleges through partnerships, both in agricultural extension and by helping them participate equitably in federal programs. Federal legislation, as currently written, requires tribal college extension programs to be administered through state Land Grant colleges. We believe state institutions must make tribal colleges equal partners and respect the unique needs, and values, of their reservations.

Further, we also strongly recommend that tribal colleges receive full funding authorized through the Land Grant Act. Although $5 million is authorized for extension programs, no funds were provided in 1996, and only $2 million were appropriated in 1997. Likewise, no funds have been released for facilities and equipment. In contrast, state Land Grant institutions received over $400 million in extension funds, and $64 million for buildings and facilities. Once again, we urge full appropriation for these valuable programs.

More broadly, the Land Grant legislation touches on issues larger than agriculture. Land is inseparably linked to cultural, spiritual, and economic issues. We agree with those in the tribal college movement who view the legislation as a vehicle to even greater social change on reservations by supporting their role as guardians of tribal homelands and natural resources.[3]

—◦—

_Third, we still urge that tribal college facilities—including libraries, science laboratories, classrooms, and residence halls—be significantly improved through federal government appropriations. We also propose that foundations, corporations, as well as state and federal government agencies, help improve facilities at tribal colleges._

We focus on facilities because the need is great, and because funding for new construction and repair is especially difficult to secure. It is a well-known maxim that money for "brick and mortar" is scarce. Yet the intellectual climate of an institution and its ability to serve the community is directly shaped by the quality of its campus and the resources it contains.

Ten years ago we found the condition of the typical tribal college's facilities to be woefully inadequate and urged immediate action. "Typically, the reports of our foundation focus on teaching and learning, not on buildings; however, tribal colleges must be an exception," we wrote.

"Most colleges are jammed for space, and struggle daily to secure needed equipment and supplies," we continued. "Such conditions are disgraceful. Facilities do make an important statement about the priorities we assign to our institutions, and the tribal college should stand, on every reservation, as a symbol of hope, with the space needed to serve adequately the educational needs of those enrolled."

Since then we have seen some improvement. Fort Berthold Community College, for example, began its life in a trailer, then moved into a series of rented storefronts along the main street in New Town, North Dakota. But by 1990 it had raised enough money through a capital campaign to construct a new building of its own on the edge of town. Today, the first phase of construction is complete and the second has begun. Likewise, Turtle Mountain College will soon begin construction of a long-anticipated new college center, leaving behind an adequate, but equally makeshift, campus. Other colleges, such as Crownpoint Institute of Technology and Fond du Lac Community College, already operate out of new and attractive campus centers.

However, site visits and student comments confirm that many pressing needs remain. Classroom and office space is at a premium and, in many cases, existing facilities are in disrepair. Peeling paint, crumbling walkways, rickety stairs, and trailers that are either too hot or too cold are all the trademarks of many tribal college campuses.

For example, a 1993 report completed for the Department of Education summarized the needs of United Tribes Technical College in Bismarck, North Dakota, an intertribal school that took over an old military base near the city's airport. New construction has turned it into a reasonably efficient college campus, but the evidence of neglect is obvious. The study found a pressing need for "major repairs and renovations to much of the campus's existing facilities, fast approaching a century of use."

It continued: "Roofs and windows are in most pressing need of repair to prevent heat loss and further deterioration of supporting brick walls. Substantial interior repairs are also needed to make dormitories for single students more habitable." The total cost for essential repairs for this one college came to over $2 million.[4]

Similar statements could be made about many other tribal colleges that, while young institutions, often inherited old and decrepit structures. But even relatively new campuses, left untended, develop their own special quirks: At Navajo Community College's campus in Tsaile, the administration building's elevator—the only one for many miles—seemed incapable of taking passengers to their intended floor during our first visit: push six, and arrive in the basement.

These weaknesses are more than inconveniences, however. Over time they directly affect the quality of instruction and an institution's ability to grow and add new academic programs. Many colleges are eager to add or expand programs in the sciences. Others are beginning to expand into four-year and graduate degree programs. All these programs offer more opportunities for students, but also tend to reveal all too clearly weaknesses in the infrastructure: small and poorly stocked libraries, inadequate classroom and laboratory space, and more.

We noted in 1988 that the Tribally Controlled Community College Assistance Act contains a provision for campus construction. The modest $1.8 million authorization cannot meet every college's needs but represents a helpful start. Yet this provision remains unfunded. Once again we urge that the full amount authorized be available for the colleges. Similarly, a $1.7 million matching grant is authorized for facilities through the Department of Agriculture. These funds—to be used for facilities related to agriculture and science education—became available after the tribal colleges were designated as Land Grant colleges. But, again, no funds have been appropriated for either 1996 or 1997.

We also described how a variety of foundations have supported the construction of new buildings and the supply of materials—from books to computers and lab equipment. The evidence of this continued support can be found across the country. The Pew Charitable Trust, for example, has supported the construction of a new library at Oglala Lakota College and the Lannan Foundation recently announced an $8.5 million initiative to build a much-needed new campus center for Sinte Gleska University.

But, without question, many pressing needs remain. We again urge that foundations and agencies within the federal government join with colleges to expand and improve campuses—providing funds for necessary new construction and, where necessary, contribute toward the repair and renovation of existing structures.

—◦—

*Fourth, we urge that connections between tribal colleges and non-Indian higher education institutions grow even stronger. We recommend that mainstream colleges and universities continue to work with tribal colleges, joining in partnerships that benefit both institutions.*

When the first tribal colleges were founded, non-Indian colleges played a mentoring, and even a parental, role. They sponsored many of the first schools, accepted credits earned by their first students, and brought credibility to a new and untested idea.

In the early years of the tribal college movement, especially, this kind of support was risky. Tribal colleges were unproven, their quality and "legitimacy" in doubt. At the same time, many educators also viewed tribal colleges as competitors and worried that they would drain valuable Indian students away from their institutions. Although tribal college leaders found allies, they also encountered skepticism and resistance.

However, in our first report we urged non-Indian institutions to reach out to tribal institutions, arguing that by helping tribal colleges, mainstream colleges and universities would also help themselves. "Rather than viewing tribal colleges simply as institutions needing assistance," we wrote, "the non-Indian four-year colleges and universities should come to understand that they have much to learn about native culture and how to support native students more successfully." Further, we noted that students who transfer from tribal colleges into mainstream institutions are more likely to succeed.

Returning a decade later, we are delighted to find a new climate. Early resistance has been replaced by a mood of cooperation, and nearly every tribal college works with non-Indian institutions through transfer agreements, faculty exchanges, research projects, and much more.

Bay Mills Community College President Martha McCleod described for us the changes she's seen. "Ten years ago I was knocking on the door of state institutions, begging for articulation recognition of this course or that course so that students could transfer," she said. "I was often frustrated. Their attitude was: 'You're either going to disappear in a while, or we hope you will.'"

But she continued: "The attitude has changed dramatically." Articulation agreements have been signed with institutions across the state, and an innovative "two-plus-two" degree program in education is now in place. Northern Michigan State University, especially, has been eager to support Bay Mills Community College, and the college has hosted the university's president, vice president, and department heads. These agreements and gestures of goodwill directly benefit students, who now know they can make a seamless transition to a variety of institutions in

Michigan and neighboring states, confident that they will not have to justify the quality of their tribal college instruction.

All other tribal colleges benefit in similar ways. We urge that institutions build on the solid foundation now established, creating even stronger ties to help students.

As a first step, we propose that a "president-to-president" relationship be established between tribal colleges and non-Indian institutions. Past experience has shown that while agreements and programs established at the departmental level are helpful, the strongest relationships are built when presidents—and other top administrators—reach out to their peers at tribal colleges.

Next, we also propose that colleges and universities then build on this new foundation by working together in other ways. Over the past ten years we have observed a variety of innovative programs that bring Indian and non-Indian colleges together, and enrich the work of both. Faculty exchange programs have brought teachers from the University of North Dakota to Turtle Mountain College, for example. Meanwhile, tribal college instructors have worked to complete graduate degrees through an innovative program with Montana State University. A biomedical research grant at that university also supported the science curriculum at Little Big Horn College. More recently, the University of North Dakota has helped United Tribes Technical College strengthen its math and science curriculum through a Hughes Foundation grant. We encourage these and many similar examples of collaboration, which can be found on every tribal college campus.

Finally, it must be acknowledged that tribal colleges have grown and matured. Increasingly, the parental relationship we described is being replaced by a partnership between equals. Indeed, tribal colleges are now being asked to be the lead partner in even major research projects. For example, two multi-million dollar grants from the National Science Foundation are being successfully administered by tribal colleges. We urge non-Indian institutions to recognize the knowledge and professionalism now found on many tribal colleges. Each has something to offer the other.

◄o►

*Fifth, we recommend that tribal colleges continue to expand their important work in preserving the arts, philosophy, science, and religious studies of their tribes. Specifically, we urge foundations and government agencies to fund programs that allow colleges to study and teach this essential knowledge.*

The study and preservation of traditional culture is a vital part of every tribal college's mission. All teach tribal languages, and most offer classes in the history and traditions of their tribe. Traditional values shape everything from campus architecture to teaching styles.

However, many within the tribal college movement believe even more should be done. Traditional knowledge is still in jeopardy and the integration of culture within the curriculum is incomplete, many say. Although colleges are eager to expand their native studies curriculum and conduct research on language and culture, a lack of money and staff has become a barrier.

At Turtle Mountain College, for example, Vice President Carol Davis describes her institution's native language programs with a mixture of pride and frustration. Determined to both record and teach the reservation's tribal languages, the college offers two sections of Chippewa Cree and Ojibwa. Recently it also hired a retired linguist who works twenty hours a week for the college, helping record the language, write a textbook, and record stories.

But these programs—as small as they are—use up precious re-sources. "We're doing this all on our own," Davis emphasized. Grant proposals to support this work have been turned down and the college does not have the staff needed to look for other sources of funding. Although the tribe worries that the language is being lost—the tribal council signaled its concern by declaring Chippewa to be the official language of the tribe—the college is unable to offer any more support.

This is a dilemma faced, to greater or lesser degrees, by many colleges. While all believe the preservation and teaching of culture is an important and unique responsibility, these programs sometimes take a back seat as a college struggles to simply survive. Meanwhile, grants that support these programs are hard to find. Language study and oral histories, especially, are valued by tribal members, but not easily funded. The importance of this study is often not appreciated by non-Indians.

In our first report, we urged foundations to support the maintenance of Indian traditions. We repeat this recommendation, and believe it is even more timely. Many tribal colleges are ready to build a curriculum that fully reflects traditional knowledge and values. They are eager, too, to expand their research role through programs that record languages, build archives, collect oral histories and, in time, apply this knowledge to modern problems.

We applaud the Lannan Foundation for its leadership. Through its Indigenous Communities Program, grants have been awarded to Blackfeet Community College for the integration of tribal history and philosophy into the curriculum. Also funded is the Ojibwa Language Institute at Bay Mills Community College, which is teaching Native American educators to speak, read, and write the Ojibwa language. Several other colleges were funded through this initiative for cultural and language programs.

The American Indian College Fund is also sponsoring an initiative to strengthen this part of the colleges' work. We are encouraged by its early success. Through this program, and through direct support to colleges, the nation, we believe, will not only better understand American Indian cultures, but also ensure that Native cultures continue to enrich America for generations to come.

❧

*Sixth, we recommend that tribal colleges enrich their curricula—and build even stronger collaboration with non-Indian institutions—through the expanded use of distance learning technology. We urge foundations and government agencies to support this initiative by providing essential "seed" money for the development of a telecommunications infrastructure and funding for the development of general education courses.*

Almost every college and university in the country is bringing technology into the classroom. From the internet to interactive video, students and teachers are working together in ways barely imagined even a decade ago. Students now routinely take classes, and even complete entire degrees, through "distance learning."

Tribal colleges, too, have made this technology a priority. Already, many are offering classes through video with non-Indian colleges, and with each other, by installing equipment that allows them to both receive and send telecourses by satellite or fiber optic lines. For example, three Montana tribal colleges—Salish Kootenai, Fort Peck, and Little Big Horn—are sharing courses with a non-Indian institution, Rocky Mountain College. These institutions offer language and culture courses in exchange for math and science instruction from the non-Indian partner. Similarly, the University of Great Falls is now offering bachelor's degrees to four Montana tribal colleges via telecommunications.

Working together, the tribal colleges also sponsor their own telecommunications project. Although still in the early stages of development, colleges within the American Indian Higher Education Consortium have already shared an anatomy and physiology class taught by an instructor at Northwest Indian College. Soon human service classes will be made available through Salish Kootenai College. In these ways, tribal colleges are sharing their expertise with other institutions and reducing the need to duplicate important but costly general education courses. "Colleges which have not had qualified instructors now are able to offer classes," explained Northwest Indian College President Bob Lorence.

Many tribal college presidents acknowledge the need for more general education courses. In addition, administrators at even some of the smaller colleges are interested in adding four-year and, in some cases, graduate degrees. Distance learning technology may offer a cost-effective path to stronger and more complete programs of study.

We therefore encourage tribal colleges and non-Indian institutions to take full advantage of this technology. Specifically, we recommend funding for three years to the tribal college telecommunications project, giving it the support needed to expand its base of participating colleges and add courses that reflect the needs of these institutions. We also recommend that tribal colleges and mainstream institutions use telecommunications to share courses that directly enrich learning for both Indian and non-Indian students.

Some tribal college presidents believe distance learning may become even more important in the future. For example, in time classes may be made available to satellite campuses on reservations not currently served by a tribal college. In addition, some envision the creation of a nontraditional tribal college without walls; classes taken electronically would lead to a recognized degree. Although these ideas are only being discussed, they do demonstrate the commitment of tribal college leaders to technology and hint at some of the opportunities it may offer in the future.

−◄○►−

*Seventh, we repeat the need for a comprehensive program of faculty development at tribal colleges.*

All colleges and universities in America expect their faculty to grow both as teachers and as scholars, but the need for professional growth is especially acute within tribal colleges.

Tribal college faculty are dedicated, but they also face significant barriers. Many are isolated from their peers, work in institutions with severely limited resources, and are given heavy teaching loads. At the same time, they also have the unique responsibility to work comfortably in two distinct cultures and serve students who arrive academically underprepared.

In our first report, we took note of a special initiative supported by the Bush Foundation that focused on faculty development at tribal colleges in North and South Dakota. At the time of our first study, the program at Turtle Mountain College, for example, was helping vocational education teachers become certified in their fields and other instructors become active within their professional organizations. The program has continued, and a recent grant to Fort Belknap College allowed faculty to pursue advanced degrees and professional training. Once again, we strongly endorse this exceptional program.

Instruction can be supported in other ways. Faculty exchanges with surrounding non-Indian institutions, summer research programs, released time for research, and more have been offered by tribal colleges— although opportunities are limited and erratic. We encourage government agencies, foundations, and non-Indian institutions to provide the support needed for this kind of professional growth.

Finally, we also encourage programs that help increase the number of Native American faculty. Currently, Indians make up 50 percent or less of instructors on most campuses. Colleges would like to hire more, but say the pool of qualified Indian teachers is small. In response, many institutions have worked informally to increase the number of Native teachers by encouraging their own students to continue their education and return as faculty. In some cases colleges even pay for the cost of educating former students, with the understanding that they would be hired after completing a professional or graduate degree. These efforts are making a difference and deserve support. Salish Kootenai College, for example, now has three former students on its faculty. The Navajo Nation provides an additional incentive with loan forgiveness programs for Native students who return to tribal colleges to teach.

—◀○▶—

*Eighth, we urge continued support of the American Indian Higher Education Consortium. Specifically, we urge increased funding for data collection and technical support to member colleges.*

The American Indian Higher Education Consortium is an essential part of the tribal college movement. By working together, college leaders are able to pool limited resources, share information, and draw greater attention to their needs and successes. The value of this work is proven: although still young, the colleges have gained federal funding and nationwide visibility.

In the first report, we recognized the significance of the consortium to the future of the colleges and urged foundations to help it grow. "With such support," we said, "the colleges would enjoy the increased visibility needed to extend public awareness and heighten legislative understanding." Our goals were modest: a Washington D.C. office and a full-time director.

This goal was soon met, and then exceeded. Today, the consortium has a full-time staff of five and works out of its own building located just outside of Washington, D.C. Funding comes from grants, along with dues paid by member colleges. The building, meanwhile, was purchased jointly by the colleges. A generous gift from the Lannan Foundation allowed the consortium to pay off its mortgage.

As we hoped, this kind of long-term support has allowed the colleges to develop a stronger voice in Washington, and even gain some new legislative successes. But the consortium has yet to fulfill its full mandate. When created, tribal college leaders believed their organization would do much more than monitor legislation. They believed it should also conduct research on behalf of the colleges, advise less experienced institutions, and promote their cause to the media. It would act as both a policy center and accrediting body, helping to define the movement and build stronger colleges.

In the past, some of this work was completed informally by member colleges. Individual presidents, working on behalf of the consortium, would, for example, agree to mentor a new college or administer a grant for all institutions. This kind of administration was cost effective, but also *ad hoc* and burdensome for individual presidents and their staff.

This approach cannot be sustained. As the movement grows, programs and services that benefit all colleges are now being centralized—not scattered among different institutions. College presidents agree their consortium must become an organization with the staff and resources needed to, on its own, secure and run grants, offer technical assistance, and conduct essential research. It must, in short, become a professional, free-standing organization.

These recommendations are made in a thoughtful strategic plan prepared by the tribal colleges. We endorse its conclusions and urge philanthropies to join together and fund, for three years or more, the expansion of the American Indian Higher Education Consortium's office in Washington, D.C. With increased staff, the consortium will be able to pursue new sources of funding within the federal government—and responsibly manage programs that serve colleges. It would be, as one staff member told us, "the eyes and ears" of the colleges.

The need for reliable data on student outcomes is a particular concern. As we described in an earlier chapter, tribal colleges are beginning to document their success. But thirty years after the founding of the first tribal colleges, far too little is known about their impact on students and communities. Even essential data on student retention, graduation, and employment is poorly tracked. Colleges cannot grow stronger—or fully answer the concerns of skeptics—without the kind of data that colleges and universities across the country are now expected to collect. Increased funding for staff dedicated to this research role is a necessary next step in the growth of the tribal colleges.

—<o>—

*Ninth, we call on foundations, corporations, the federal government, and individuals to continue their support of the American Indian College Fund.*

The American Indian College Fund represents one of the great successes of the tribal college movement. Created in 1989 primarily to raise private sector funds for student scholarships, it has grown beyond expectations and is helping build stronger institutions and greater public awareness.

In our first report, we made brief note of a "tribal college endowment" and argued for its value. "American higher education discovered long ago that quality cannot be achieved if an institution is forced to live from hand to mouth, with no stability in support," we wrote. "This is just as true for a new college as for our oldest and most prestigious institutions."

At the time, the college fund was a promising but untested idea. Could the colleges build a credible fund-raising institution? Would its message be heard? Would the nation respond?

The answer, nearly a decade later, is a resounding "yes." Since its inception, annual giving to the fund has grown from less than $160,000 in 1989 to over $5.4 million in 1995. In that year the total amount raised was nearly $18 million. Total endowment funds now exceed $5 million. In addition, money distributed annually to each college for student scholarships and operating support has grown from a mere $800 per school to over $50,000.

Tribal colleges, like mainstream institutions, have their own endowments, although most are quite small. Several colleges also pursue their own fund-raising campaigns. But without question, the American Indian College Fund, which was developed by the tribal college consortium and is directed by a board dominated by tribal college presidents, offers the greatest hope for financial security. By working together, the colleges have created an organization that provides the visibility and credibility that no college working on its own can duplicate.

We are also impressed by the quality of the Fund's leadership and its ability to attract national leaders willing to work on behalf of the tribal colleges. Senator Ben Nighthorse Campbell, of Colorado, is on the board of directors and has authored numerous articles describing the needs of tribal colleges. Public service ads for both print and television have been developed *pro bono* by the Wieden & Kennedy advertising agency, best know for its "Just Do It" Nike shoe ads. Currently, it is also working with the Pendleton blanket company to produce a special line of blankets which would earn income for the colleges.

With its success, the college fund has revised its fund-raising goals and is finding new ways to support the colleges directly. An initial target of $5 million in endowment funds—already met—has been raised to $15 million. In addition, the AICF hopes to double its annual scholarship distribution to each college, from about $50,000 to $100,000 and to mount a multi-year, multi-million dollar campaign. Ten years ago these goals may have seemed impossible; now they are merely ambitious.

In another initiative, the AICF is working directly to support the study of American Indian culture at each college; a separate endowment was created to support Native American Studies programs. Established with a $750,000 matching grant from the National Endowment for the Humanities, the total endowment has grown to close to $2 million.

We share with the colleges their pride in these accomplishments. The success of this effort not only provides tangible support to the colleges but it also proves once again the ability of the colleges to overcome barriers, work together, and manage effective institutions. We therefore emphatically renew our commitment to this effort and urge the nation to generously support the fund, helping it meet its goals.

◄○►

*Tenth, we encourage continued funding of the journal* Tribal College.

We also renew our commitment to *Tribal College: Journal of American Indian Higher Education.* This quarterly publication was started by the colleges just as we were finishing work on the original Carnegie Foundation tribal college report. At the time, it was only a twenty-four page journal with a circulation of less than one thousand, but it satisfied a genuine need and we urged support for the effort.

In that era, especially, the colleges were isolated from the rest of the nation. They had few opportunities to learn from each other, or share their story with policymakers, foundations, and educators. A journal, we felt, provided an obvious, and relatively inexpensive, solution. "This publication will strengthen the network of institutions, provide for intellectual exchange, and give a sense of identity as well," we predicted.

Today, the journal looks quite different. Professionally edited and de-signed, it is filled with well-written articles, research, commentary, and reviews. For most years, its shoestring budget came from the colleges and a patchwork of small grants. A more generous grant from the Lannan Foundation in 1994 helped it expand; a full-time editor and office manager now take responsibility for the *Tribal College* journal.

The journal is still one of the smallest activities supported by the colleges—its budget and staff are tiny compared to the American Indian Higher Education Consortium and the American Indian College Fund. But its impact can be felt throughout the colleges and complements many of this report's key recommendations.

The journal has, for example, addressed the need for research by publishing scholarship on subjects ranging from student achievement to the role of America's Colonial colleges in Indian education. It has, on its own, devised a special initiative to study the research needs of reservations and sponsored a conference on the role of Native American scholarship. Meanwhile, administrators can turn to it for articles on effective teaching, assessment, and endowment investing—supporting our call for faculty development and leadership training. In addition, both the consortium and college fund use the journal to strengthen their work; copies are distributed widely on Capitol Hill and mailed to donors.

The journal also reaches into classrooms. Recently, it published an attractive anthology of student writing, and it also supports a special "student edition" filled with essays, stories, and research from tribal college students around the country. One writing instructor even organizes her whole class around the journal's upcoming themes, calling it "a mentor on the desk."

Unlike many association-sponsored journals, *Tribal College* is not primarily a public relations organ. Instead, as its editor recently explained, it "is targeted first at the tribal college audience. They are, after all, our *raison d'etre* . . ." By stressing this part of its mission, the journal has become a serious, scholarly forum. Indeed, we relied extensively on the journal while completing research for this report.

Publications have, as a general rule, an uncertain future. The life of the journal *Tribal College* is especially tenuous. Although it is working successfully to increase its base of paid subscribers and advertising, it continues to need outside support. We strongly urge that foundations join to support this publication, allowing it to serve the colleges during this time of growth.

WE CONCLUDE with a recommendation to the nation and, especially, to America's non-Indian schools.

We began our first study with only the most rudimentary under-standing of contemporary Indian societies. Like many Americans, we found ourselves largely ignorant of their histories, strengths, and needs. Native Americans loom large in our nation's imagination, and reservation land occupies large blocks of the American West, but real understanding was absent.

Throughout our studies, members of the tribal college community and other tribal leaders graciously welcomed us into their world and answered our many questions. We are grateful for the time they devoted to our education, but came to understand that it is, for them, a familiar task. Each time they go to Congress, a state legislature, a federal courtroom, or a newspaper reporter, they become teachers. They must continually explain who they are as a people and what their place is in the nation, always struggling to push away stereotypes that distort the truth and hinder their progress.

So while we describe the educational needs of Indians in this report, we believe Indian education should come to mean not just the education of Indians, but also education *about* Indians. Marjane Ambler, editor of the *Tribal College* journal reported this problem eloquently in a recent issue, and went on to write about the impact America's ignorance has on the lives of Indians:

> I have yet to meet anyone who was taught about treaties or tribal sovereignty in a high school civics class when they learned about federal, state and local governments. When conflicts arise it is not a time for education. As states and tribes battle over taxation, water rights, or gaming compacts, citizens tend to be polarized, not informed by the debate.

We therefore conclude our study with the hope that Native Americans will be given a stronger place in the curriculum of America's schools. The goal should be more than increased "sensitivity" or awareness of "diversity." Rather, we propose that all students, by the completion of high school, leave with three pieces of essential knowledge.

First, we believe every student should have developed an understanding of the rich Native American heritage. They should explore the diversity of tribal cultures and their place on the continent before the arrival of Europeans. As a people, Native Americans developed unique and complex societies. This should be the foundation of any course that examines America's history.

Second, we encourage educators to remind students that Indians are a contemporary people. Students should learn that traditional values remain. But it is important to also show how Indians are participating fully in American society as doctors, politicians, teachers, artists, and more. Simple notions of Indians living in isolation, clinging only to the past, must be set aside after even a brief examination of modern reservation life.

Finally, every student should be aware that Native Americans fill a unique place in the nation's body of law. As the original inhabitants, they are identified individually within the Constitution and maintain relationships with the federal government defined by treaties and a notion of "trust responsibility." Their relationship with the nation, and the government, remains distinct.

At the conclusion of our first report on tribal colleges, we said the idea of Indian-controlled higher education "is both valid and overdue." As we complete this new study, we find that the evidence of the success of these Indian higher education institutions is clear. Tribal colleges are continuing to quietly serve their communities by reclaiming and passing on Indian culture, and by creating opportunity and renewing hope. We are convinced that, with ongoing support, they will continue to enrich the lives of students and tribal societies, and indeed will enrich the whole nation.

# APPENDIX

# *Tribally Controlled Colleges*

Bay Mills Community College
Route 1, Box 315-A
Brimley, Michigan 49715
(906) 248-3354 Fax: (906) 248-3351

Blackfeet Community College
P.O. Box 819
Browning, Montana 59417
(406) 338-7755 Fax: (406) 338-7808

Cheyenne River Community College
P.O. Box 220
Eagle Butte, South Dakota 57625
(605) 964-8635 Fax: (605) 964-1144

College of the Menominee Nation
P.O. Box 1179
Keshena, Wisconsin 54135
(715) 799-4921 Fax: (715) 799-1308

Crownpoint Institute of Technology
P.O. Box 849
Crownpoint, New Mexico 87313
(505) 786-5851 Fax: (505) 786-5644
email: citdl@nm—us.campus.mci.net

D-Q University
P.O. Box 409
Davis, California 95617
(916) 758-0470 Fax: (916) 758-4891
http://wheel.dcn.davis.ca.us/~jariggen/
    dqhome.html

Dull Knife Memorial College
P.O. Box 98
Lame Deer, Montana 59043
(406) 477-6215 Fax: (406) 477-6219
email: afpang@ww.dkmc.cc.mt.us

Fond du Lac Community College
2101 14th Street
Cloquet, Minnesota 55720
(218) 879-0800 Fax: (218) 879-0814
email: ljbriggs@asab.fdl.cc.mn.us

Fort Belknap College
P.O. Box 159
Harlem, Montana 59526
(406) 353-2607 Fax: (406) 353-2898

Fort Berthold Community College
P.O. Box 490
New Town, North Dakota 58763
(701) 627-3665 Fax: (701) 627-3609

Fort Peck Community College
P.O. Box 575
Poplar, Montana 59255
(406) 768-5551 Fax: (406) 768-5552

Lac Courte Oreilles Ojibwa Community
    College
R.R. 2, Box 2357
Hayward, Wisconsin 54843
(715) 634-4790 Fax: (715) 634-5049
email: lcoocc1@win.bright.net

Leech Lake Tribal College
Route 3, Box 100
Cass Lake, Minnesota 56633
(218) 335-2828 Fax: (218) 335-7845

Little Big Horn College
P.O. Box 370
Crow Agency, Montana 59022
(406) 638-2228 Fax: (406) 638-7213

Little Hoop Community College
P.O. Box 209
Fort Totten, North Dakota 58335
(701) 766-4415 Fax: (701) 766-4077

Little Priest College
P.O. Box 270
Winnebago, Nebraska 68071
(402) 878-2380 Fax: (402) 878-2355

Navajo Community College
P.O. Box 126
Tsaile, Arizona 86556
(520) 724-3311 Fax: (520) 724-3327

Nebraska Indian Community College
P.O. Box 752
Winnebago, Nebraska 68071
(402) 878-2414 Fax: (402) 878-2522

Northwest Indian College
2522 Kwina Road
Bellingham, Washington 98226
(360) 676-2772 Fax: (360) 738-0136
email: boblorn@aol.com

Oglala Lakota College
P.O. Box 490
Kyle, South Dakota 57752
(605) 455-2321 Fax: (605) 455-2787

Salish Kootenai College
P.O. Box 117
Pablo, Montana 59855
(406) 675-4800 Fax: (406) 675-4801
email: joe_mcdonald@skc.edu

Sinte Gleska University
P.O. Box 490
Rosebud, South Dakota 57570
(605) 747-2263 Fax: (605) 747-2098

Sisseton Wahpeton Community College
P.O. Box 689
Sisseton, South Dakota 57262
(605) 698-3966 Fax: (605) 698-3132
email: jderby@daknet.com

Southwest Indian Polytechnic Institute
Box 10146-9169
Coors Road NW
Albuquerque, New Mexico 87184
(505) 897-5347 Fax: (505) 897-5343
email: ce@kafka.sipi.tec.nm.us

Sitting Bull College
HC 1, Box 4
Fort Yates, North Dakota 58538
(701) 854-3861 Fax: (701) 854-3403

Stone Child Community College
Rocky Boy Route, Box 1082
Box Elder, Montana 59521
(406) 395-4313 Fax: (406) 395-4836

Turtle Mountain Community College
P.O. Box 340
Belcourt, North Dakota 58316
(701) 477-5605 Fax: (701) 477-5028
email: cartym@aol.com

United Tribes Technical College
3315 University Drive
Bismarck, North Dakota 58504
(701) 255-3285 Fax: (701) 255-1844
email: dmgipp@aol.com

# NOTES

# NOTES

INTRODUCTION

1. The terms Native American, American Indian and Indian are used interchangeably throughout the report. These remain the most common forms of identification for the indigenous peoples of the lower forty-eight states.

2. American Indian Higher Education Consortium, "Tribal Colleges," fact sheet, Alexandria, Va.

3. Patricia Porter McNamara, *American Indians in U.S. Higher Education* (Los Angeles, Calif.: Higher Education Research Institute, 1984), 104.

4. Deborah J. Carter and Reginald Wilson, *Minorities in Higher Education: Twelfth Annual Status Report* (Washington, D.C.: American Council on Education, 1993), 4.

5. Deborah J. Carter and Reginald Wilson, *Minorities in Higher Education: Fourteenth Annual Status Report* (Washington, D.C.: American Council on Education, 1996), 27.

6. Paul Boyer, "The Model Scholar," *Tribal College: Journal of American Indian Higher Education*, vol. 4 (Winter 1992–93), 20–22.


CHAPTER I:  *A History of Mis-education*

1. Alice C. Fletcher, *Indian Education and Civilization: A Report Prepared in Answer to Senate Resolution of February 23, 1885* (Washington, D.C.: Government Printing Office, 1888), 32–33.

2. *Ibid.*, 33.

3. *Ibid.*, 53.

4. *Ibid.*, 54.

5. *Ibid.*

6. Francis Paul Prucha, *The Indians in American Society from the Revolutionary War to the Present* (Berkeley: University of California Press, 1985), 6–8.

7. *Ibid.*, 6.

8.  *Ibid.*, 12.

9.  Benjamin Franklin, *Two Tracts, Information to Those Who Would Remove to America and Remarks Concerning the Savages of North America*, 3rd ed. (London: 1794), 28–29; cited in Estelle Fuchs and Robert J. Havinghurst, *To Live on This Earth: American Indian Education* (Garden City, N.Y.: Doubleday, 1973), 3.

10. Frederick Law Olmsted, *A Journey Through Texas* (1857; reprint, with a foreword by Larry McMurtry, Austin: University of Texas Press, 1978), 289–90.

11. Charles Maclaren, *Werner Encyclopedia*, vol. I, 602, 604; cited in *The Indian in America's Past*, ed. J. Forbes (Englewood Cliffs, N.J.: Prentice-Hall, 1964), 17.

12. Richard Henry Pratt, *Battlefield and Classroom: Four Decades with the American Indian, 1968–1904*, ed. and with an introduction by Robert M. Utley (Lincoln, Nebr.: University of Nebraska Press, 1987), 335.

13. Elaine Eastman, *Pratt: The Red Man's Moses* (Norman, Okla.: University of Oklahoma, 1935), 85.

14. *Ibid.*

15. Ida S. Patterson, *Montana Memories: The Life of Emma Magee in the Rocky Mountain West, 1866–1950* (Pablo, Mont.: Salish Kootenai Community College, 1981), 90–91.

16. *Tentative Course of Study for United States Indian Schools* (Washington, D.C.: Government Printing Office, 1915), 5.

17. Francis Paul Prucha, *Americanizing the American Indian* (Cambridge: Harvard University Press, 1973), 257–59.

18. Margaret Connell Szasz, *Education and the American Indian: The Road to Self-Determination Since 1928* (Albuquerque, N. Mex.: University of New Mexico Press, 1974), 10.

19. Francis Paul Prucha, *The Indians in American Society*, 51.

20. Lewis Meriam, *The Problem of Indian Administration* (Baltimore, Md.: Johns Hopkins Press, 1928), 3–5.

21. *New York Times*, 23 May 1928.

22. Lewis Meriam, 32.

23. "The Right To Be An Indian," *New York Times*, 2 December 1928.

24. John Collier, *Indians of the Americas*, abridged (New York: Mentor, 1947), 155.

25. *Ibid.*

26. Margaret Connell Szasz, 78.


CHAPTER 2:     *The Founding of Tribal Colleges*

1. Steven Crum, "The Idea of an Indian College or University in Twentieth Century America Before the Founding of Navajo Community College in 1968," *Tribal College: Journal of American Indian Higher Education*, vol. 1 (Summer 1989), 20.

2. August Breuniger to Dr. Carlos Montezuma, 2 March 1911, *Carlos Montezuma Papers* (State Historical Society of Wisconsin, 1975, microfilm ed.), 20.

3. Steven Crum, "The Hoover Administration's 'New Era': American Indian Higher Education, 1929–1933" (draft chapter for unpublished book, 1987), 8.

4. *Ibid.*, 13.

5. Steven Crum, "Crow Warrior," *Tribal College: Journal of American Indian Higher Education*, vol. 1 (Spring 1990), 19–23.

6. Guy B. Senese, *Self-Determination and the Social Education* (New York: Praeger, 1991), 3.

7. Kenneth R. Philp, ed., *Indian Self-Rule: First-Hand Accounts of Indian-White Relations from Roosevelt to Reagan* (Salt Lake City, Utah: Howe Brothers, 1986), 141.

8. Janine Pease-Windy Boy, "The Tribally Controlled Community College Act of 1978: An Expansion of Federal Indian Trust Responsibilities" (Ph.D. diss., Montana State University, 1994), 23.

9. Cited in S. Lyman Tyler, *A History of Indian Policy* (Washington, D.C.: United States Department of the Interior, Bureau of Indian Affairs, 1973), 200.

10. Francis Paul Prucha, *The Indian in American Society from the Revolutionary War to the Present* (Berkeley, Calif.: University of California Press, 1985), 83–84.

11. S. Lyman Tyler, 214.

12. Frederick Rudolph, *The American College and University: A History* (New York: Knopf, 1962), 487.

13. Wayne Stein, *A History of the Tribally Controlled Community Colleges: 1968–1978* (Ph.D. diss., Washington State University, 1988), 33.

14. Peter Nabokov, ed., *Native American Testimony: A Chronicle of Indian-White Relations from Prophecy to the Present, 1492–1992* (New York: Viking, 1991), 333.

15. Estelle Fuchs and Robert J. Havinghurst, *To Live on This Earth: American Indian Education* (Garden City, N.Y.: Doubleday, 1973), 260.

16. Margaret Connell Szaz, *Education and the American Indian: The Road to Self-Determination Since 1928* (Albuquerque, N. Mex.: University of New Mexico Press, 1974), 10.

17. Wayne Stein, 39.

18. Estelle Fuchs and Robert J. Havinghurst, 270.

19. Wayne Stein, 38.

20. *Ibid.*

21. Kenneth R. Philp, 203.

CHAPTER 3:    *An Overview of Tribal Colleges*

1. Turtle Mountain Community College, *Self Study*, 1993, 20; Gerald Slater and Michel O'Donnell, "What Tribal Colleges Teach," *Tribal College: Journal of American Indian Higher Education*, Vol. 7 (Summer 1995), 39–40.

2. Kyle Patterson Cross and Phillip V. Shortman, "Tribal College Faculty: The Demographics," *Tribal College: Journal of American Indian Higher Education*, vol. 7 (Summer 1995), 36.

3. The Carnegie Foundation for the Advancement of Teaching, Survey of Tribal College Students, 1995. This survey was completed by 1,614 currently enrolled students from 24 tribal colleges nationwide. Survey instruments were prepared by The Carnegie Foundation and distributed to students by staff or faculty of each participating college. While results are not based on a random sample, it is the largest, most comprehensive survey of tribal college students yet completed. Unless otherwise cited, all data on students were gathered from this survey.

4. Kyle Patterson Cross and Philip V. Shortman, 35.

5. Georgianna Tiger, *American Indian Higher Education Consortium Congressional Testimony*, March 13, 1995, 3.

6. Paul Boyer, "Tribal College of the Future," *Tribal College: Journal of American Indian Higher Education*, vol. 7 (Summer 1995), 11.

7. American Indian Higher Education Consortium, *Overview of the 1978 Tribal Colleges Act*, March 1996.

8. American Indian Higher Education Consortium.


CHAPTER 4:    *Tribal Colleges in Context*

1. Russell Thornton, *American Indian Holocaust and Survival* (Norman, Okla.: University of Oklahoma Press, 1987), 32.

2. George Catlin, *Letters and Notes on the Manners Customs and Condition of North American Indians Vol. 1* (1844; reprint, New York: Dover, 1973), 10; cited in Patricia Nelson Limerick, *The Legacy of Conquest* (New York: W.W. Norton, 1987), 183.

3. Patricia Nelson Limerick, 187.

4. J. Lee Humfreville, *Twenty Years Among Our Savage Indians* (Hartford, Conn.: Hartford Publishing Co., 1897), 51; cited in Jack D. Forbes, ed., *The Indians in America's Past* (Englewood Cliffs, N.J.: Prentice-Hall, 1964), 79.

5. From an undated UPI/Bettman Archives Photo, published in *Tribal College: Journal of American Indian Higher Education*, vol. 7 (Summer 1995), 12.

6. Edgar S. Cahn, ed., *Our Brother's Keeper: The Indian in White America* (New York: New Community Press, 1969), 2.

7. "Casinos Alone Cannot End Poverty in Indian Country," *First Nations Economic Development: Business Alert*, January/February 1995, 7.

8. Schuyler Houser, "Mending the Circle: Peer Group Lending for Micro Enterprise Development in Tribal Communities," in *Rural Development Strategy*, ed. David W. Sears and J. Norman Reid (Chicago: Nelson-Hall, Inc., 1995), 204–231.

9. Gerald "Carty" Monette, Turtle Mountain College, personal communication, 7 August 1996.

10. Cheryl Crazy Bull, Sicangu Enterprise Center, personal communication, 17 July 1996.

11. Marjane Ambler, "The Wealth of (Indian) Nations," *Tribal College: Journal of American Indian Higher Education*, vol. 4 (Fall 1992), 10.

12. "Tourism Supports Economic Development on Crow Reservation," *Tribal College: Journal of American Indian Higher Education*, vol. 6 (Winter 1994–95), 44–45.

13. "Tourism Supports Economic Development on Crow Reservation."

14. Gerald "Carty" Monette.

15. Cited in Marjane Ambler, "The Long Tradition of Defying Selfishness," *Tribal College: Journal of American Indian Higher Education*, vol. 7 (Winter 1995–96), 8.

16. Jerry Reynold, First Nations Development Institute, personal communication, 18 July 1996.

17. First Nations Development Institute, *A Vision for Tribal Self-Reliance* (Fredericksburg, Va.: First Nations Development Institute, 1995).

18. Schuyler Houser, Salish Kootenai College, Spokane College Campus, personal communication, 6 August 1996.

19. Stephen Cornell, *The Return of the Native: American Indian Political Resurgence* (New York: Oxford University Press, 1988), 210.

20. James Shanley, Fort Peck Community College, personal communication, 19 August 1996.

21. Stephen Cornell, 211.

22. "Casinos Alone Cannot End Poverty," 7.

23. Clifford LaFramboise and Marie Watt, "Mixed Media: Blending the Traditional and Contemporary in Indian Art," *Tribal College Journal of American Indian Higher Education*, vol. 3 (Summer 1993), 9.

24. "Language Immersion Schools Begin," *Indian Country Today*, August 5–12, 1996.

25. Harold L. Hodgkinson with Janice Hamilton Outtz and Anita M. Obarakpor, *The Demographics of American Indians* (Washington, D.C.: Institute for Educational Leadership, Inc., 1990), 15–19.

26. "The Forgotten Minority: Delivering Health Care to American Indians," *Northwest Report*, January 1993, 26.

27. George Hardeen, "Hogans in Hospitals: Navajo Patients Want the Best of Both Worlds," *Tribal College: Journal of American Indian Higher Education*, vol. 5 (Winter 1994–95), 20–21.

28. Marjane Ambler, "Taking Care of Our Own: Training Indians to Heal Indians," *Tribal College: Journal of American Indian Higher Education*, vol. 5 (Winter 1994–95), 16.

29. Nancy Butteffield, Paul Boyer, and Jennifer Gray Reddish, "Cultures in Recovery," *Tribal College: Journal of American Indian Higher Education*, vol. 6 (Winter 1994–95), 9.

30. Amanda War Bonnett, "Mothers Want Change in Alcohol Laws," *Indian Country Today*, August 12–19, 1996.

CHAPTER 5:   *Fulfilling the Vision*

1. Jack Forbes, *Native American Higher Education: The Struggle for the Creation of D-Q University 1960–1971* (Davis, Calif.: D-Q University Press, 1985), 47.

2. Jasjit Minhas, La Courte Oreilles Ojibwa College, personal communication, 22 October 1996.

3. Gerald "Carty" Monette, Turtle Mountain Community College, personal communication, 31 December 1996.

4. Schuyler Houser, *Underfunded Miracles: Tribal Colleges* (Indian Nations at Risk Congressional paper #8: Tribal Colleges, 1992).

5. Joseph McDonald, Salish Kootenai College, personal communication, 22 November 1996.

6. Danielle Sanders, "Cultural Conflicts: An Important Factor in the Academic Failure of American Indian Students," *Journal of Multicultural Counseling and Development* (April 1987), 86.

7. David Begay and Nancy Maryboy, Navajo Community College, personal communication, 16 December 1996.

8. Gerald "Carty" Monette, personal communication.

9. Gerald "Carty" Monette, "Follow-up Study of the Graduates of An American Indian Tribally Controlled Community College" (Ph.D. diss., University of North Dakota, 1995), 117–18.

10. Membership Report, Fort Belknap College, *1996.* Data presented at the American Indian Higher Education Consortium Fall Board Meeting at Rapid City, South Dakota, 7 October 1996.

11. Membership Report, data presented at the American Indian Higher Education Consortium Fall Board Meeting, Rapid City, S. Dak., Oct. 7, 1996.

12. Oglala Lakota College, *Dare to Dream* (Kyle, S. Dak.: Oglala Lakota College, 1996), 8.

13. *Ibid.*

14. "Giving Families a Head Start," *Tribal College: Journal of American Indian Higher Education*, vol. 6 (Summer 1994), 6.

15. Annette T. Brown, "Local Access, Local Control," *Tribal College: Journal of American Indian Higher Education*, vol. 6 (Summer 1994), 24–25.

16. Jonny Arlee, abstract of paper presented at the Native Research and

Scholarship Symposium sponsored by the *Tribal College Journal*, Orcas Island, Washington, 21–22 July 1996.

CHAPTER 6:    *Recommendations for Action*

1. U.S. Congress, Senate Hearings Before the Select Committee on Indian Affairs, 20 March 1996, 1.

2. *Tribal College Executive Order*, American Indian Higher Education Consortium, Alexandria, Va., undated position paper, 4.

3. Phil Baird, United Tribes Technical College, personal communication, 7 November 1996.

4. Lorelei Brush, Kerry Traylor, Michael O' Leary, *Assessment of Training and Housing Needs Within Tribally Controlled Postsecondary Vocational Institutions* (Washington, D.C.: U.S. Department of Education, Office of Policy and Planning, February 1993), 4.

# INDEX

# INDEX